CONTEMPORARY BROADWAY AUDITION MEN'S EDITION

15 Songs in Full, Authentic Editions, Plus "16-Bar" Audition Versions

CONTEMPORARY BROADWAY AUDITION

To access recorded accompaniments online, visit:
www.halleonard.com/mylibrary

Enter Code
3064-9626-1825-4253

ISBN 978-1-5400-1201-2

HAL•LEONARD®

7777 W. BLUEMOUND RD. P.O. BOX 13819 MILWAUKEE, WI 53213

Visit Hal Leonard Online at
www.halleonard.com

PREFACE

It's become a custom in professional circles, community theatres and even large universities for a "16-bar" version of a song to be required for auditions. This means around 30 seconds of music. But what if they like you and say, "Sing the whole song." This collection of songs has you ready for that situation.

Not only that, it would be crazy to learn a 16-Bar excerpt of a song without learning the whole song first. Only after knowing the entire song very well, and understanding its meaning, as well as the character singing the song, can you possibly succeed in performing an excerpt of a song.

All the songs in this collection are from contemporary musical theatre, dating from 2002 to 2017. Songs were chosen that are particularly good for auditions, coming from a strong character. The excerpt has been carefully selected to show off the voice, with a brief but practical beginning and ending.

It is very, very important for you to practice starting a 16-Bar excerpt over and over. The last thing you want is for the pianist to start and you are not ready, or are not sure where to come in. That's a very bad first impression.

Break a leg!

The Editors

CONTENTS

Full Version	16-Bar Version	SONG TITLE	SHOW TITLE
8	22	Dust and Ashes [3] [*]	*Natasha, Pierre & The Great Comet of 1812*
24	34	Fight the Dragons [3] [***]	*Big Fish*
36	44	Her Voice [3] [*]	*The Little Mermaid*
46	50	I Am Aldolpho [2] [***]	*The Drowsy Chaperone*
52	63	I Believe [5] [**]	*The Book of Mormon*
65	74	If I Didn't Believe in You [1] [**]	*The Last Five Years*
76	82	Proud of Your Boy [6] [***]	*Aladdin*
83	90	Right Before My Eyes [6] [***]	*Ever After*
92	104	Run Away with Me [6] [***]	*The Unauthorized Autobiography of Samantha Brown*
107	114	Sibella [3] [*]	*A Gentleman's Guide to Love & Murder*
116	121	Still [5] [**]	*Anastasia*
122	130	Take a Chance on Me [4] [***]	*Little Women*
133	146	Waving Through a Window [3] [*]	*Dear Evan Hansen*
148	156	What Do I Need with Love [5] [*]	*Thoroughly Modern Millie*
157	164	You'll Be Back [5] [**]	*Hamilton*

Pianists on the Full Version Recordings:
[1] Jason Robert Brown   [2] Brian Dean   [3] Brendan Fox   [4] Christopher Ruck   [5] Ruben Piirainen   [6] Richard Walters

Pianist on the 16-Bar Version Recordings:
[*] Brendan Fox   [**] Ruben Piirainen   [***] Richard Walters

The price of this publication includes access to companion recorded accompaniments online,
for download or streaming, using the unique code found on the title page.
Visit **www.halleonard.com/mylibrary** and enter the access code.

ABOUT THE SHOWS AND SONGS

ALADDIN (Broadway 2014)
Music by Alan Menken
Lyrics by Howard Ashman, Tim Rice, and Chad Beguelin

Aladdin is based on the 1992 Disney animated feature of the same name. In the fictional Middle Eastern city of Agrabah, Aladdin is orphaned and homeless, and survives by stealing food from street vendors. However, he vows to mend his ways at the beginning of the musical to stop being a "worthless street rat" and to make his deceased mother **"Proud of Your Boy."** This is one of three songs with lyrics by Howard Ashman not used in the film but incorporated into the stage musical score.

ANASTASIA (Broadway 2017)
Music by Stephen Flaherty
Lyrics by Lynn Ahrens

Though the musical is based on the 1997 animated film of the same name, 16 additional songs, new characters, new subplots, and a change of setting for the second act make this adaptation of *Anastasia* almost a completely new production. Anya is a young orphaned woman has no memory of her past. She meets two con artists who have a scheme to dress a young woman up as the Grand Duchess Anastasia, who is rumored to have survived a coup that murdered the Russian royal family ten years earlier. The con artists, Dmitry and Vlad, choose Anya because of her resemblance to Anastasia. They begin coaching her on royal etiquette in hopes they can use Anya to extort the only surviving member of the family, the expatriated Dowager Empress, who is living in Paris. However, Anya and Dmitry begin to suspect that Anya actually might be Anastasia. The three are pursued across Russia on the way to Paris by Bolshevik General Gleb bent on carrying out his father's work of exterminating the royal family. The General also has feelings for Anya and questions his loyalties in **"Still."** In Paris, after much distrust and questioning, it is finally determined that Anya is the Grand Duchess Anastasia and she is reunited with her grandmother. Anastasia and Dmitry fall in love and return to Russia.

BIG FISH (Broadway 2013)
Music and Lyrics by Andrew Lippa

The big-hearted musical *Big Fish* is based on the original 1998 novel by Daniel Wallace, as well as the 2003 film adaptation by John August (who also wrote the book for the musical). The main characters are Edward Bloom, his wife Sandra and their son William. Edward has spent his life regaling Will with fanciful tales of his past, including a story about a giant fish that jumped into a man's arms after Edward taught the fisherman to catch fish by doing the "Alabama Stomp." Scenes jump between the present and the past, interspersed with Edward's fanciful tales. In a flashback scene near the beginning of Act II when Will was a young boy, he is upset when his father tells him he has to go away for a while because of his work as a traveling salesman. Edward calms him and tells Will he has to be brave and carry on while he's away, and inspires the boy by singing **"Fight the Dragons."** Edward becomes seriously ill with cancer and dies. By Edward's funeral Will has learned that all of his father's tales were in fact based in truth.

THE BOOK OF MORMON (Broadway 2011)
Music and Lyrics by Robert Lopez, Trey Parker, and Matt Stone

South Park creators Trey Parker and Matt Stone lampoon some stereotypes about the Mormon faith in the hit musical *The Book of Mormon*. Elders Cunningham and Price end up in Uganda for their two years of compulsory missionary service where they begin to proselytize a small village. Fear of the warlord of the region keeps many of the population from paying much attention to the missionaries. However, when women of the village are threatened with genital mutilation, some natives begin to consider the message of the Ladder Day Saints as a more agreeable option. In the second act, Elder Price meets with the warlord and sings about his respect to the doctrines of the church in **"I Believe."** The unpersuaded warlord inserts the *Book of Mormon* into the missionary's rear end. Both missionaries grow increasingly frustrated by perceived failure and both in some way abandon their original mission, Price fleeing to Orlando and Cunningham beginning to incorporate elements of fantasy into his message. The new altered version of the Mormon faith is appealing to the villagers and many decide to be baptized. Condemnation from the church for heretical teachings as well as death threats from the warlord push the community toward the acceptance of spiritual stories as universal metaphors that encourage positive personal and social behavior as they work toward paradise on earth.

THE DROWSY CHAPERONE (Broadway 2006; London 2007)
Music and Lyrics by Lisa Lambert, Greg Morrison

This show-within-a-show features a rather sour character simply called the Man in Chair, who escapes his depression by obsessively playing an old recording of a 1928 musical, *The Drowsy Chaperone*. Its story is of an actress, Janet Van De Graaff (Sutton Foster in the original cast), indulgent in vanity, engaged to a man she has only recently met. The show, characters, story and songs are an affectionate send-up of stage and screen clichés. Through it all the Man in Chair gets swept up in the action, and frequently comments to the audience. At one point a Latin lothario, Aldolpho, has been enlisted to seduce Janet to stop her wedding. He enters her room, which is currently occupied by Janet's middle-aged, heavy-drinking Chaperone. Thinking the older women is Janet, the he introduces himself in **"I Am Aldolpho."**

EVER AFTER (2015)
Music by Zina Goldrich
Lyrics by Marcy Heisler

Ever After received its world premiere in 2015 at the Paper Mill Playhouse, a major regional theater in Milburn, New Jersey, just across the river from Manhattan. The musical, based on the 1998 film starring Drew Barrymore, is a retelling of the classic Cinderella story, this time with a more empowered heroine. As in the traditional story, Danielle (the Cinderella character) is left with her cruel stepmother and stepsister following her father's death. In **"Right Before My Eyes"** Danielle struggles with the truth as Prince Henry declares she is the love of his life, and vows to tell the world at the masque.

A GENTLEMAN'S GUIDE TO LOVE & MURDER (Broadway 2013)

Music by Steven Lutvak
Lyrics by Robert L. Freedman and Steven Lutvak

The musical comedy *A Gentleman's Guide to Love & Murder* is based on the 1907 novel *Israel Rank: The Autobiography of a Criminal* by Roy Horniman. The style of the light-hearted musical recalls operetta and the British music hall. The main character is Monty Navarro, a young man in London who grew up in poverty, but is informed following the death of his mother that she was a member of the noble D'Ysquith family, and that he is ninth in line to be the Earl of Highhurst. He schemes to murder those relatives who stand in his way in a series of what appear to be freak accidents. Monty is in love with Sibella. She is also in love with Monty, but she will not marry him because he is poor. Instead she decides marries the likelier prospect Lionel Holland. Despite being married, Monty and Sibella carry on an affair. At the beginning of Act II Monty sings **"Sibella"** about his continued affection for her. He is soon arrested for the one murder he didn't commit. More plot twists occur before Monty's release from prison at the end of the show.

HAMILTON (Off-Broadway 2015; Broadway 2015)

Music and Lyrics by Lin-Manuel Miranda

Hamilton combines American history with hip-hop, and tells the story of Founding Father Alexander Hamilton's life from the onset of his career until his death. Early in the show, in 1776 the spirit of revolution is surging in the British American colonies. A loyal royalist preaches against the revolution, rebuked by the fervent Hamilton. A message arrives from King George III of England, reminding the colonists that he will send troops if he suspects the revolution is getting out hand, and suggesting that they will soon submit to the English monarch again. His song, **"You'll Be Back,"** shows his overconfidence, cluelessness and insouciant insensitivity. The story continues deep into American history of the Revolutionary War years and after, culminating in the death of Hamilton in a famous duel with his rival Aaron Burr.

THE LAST FIVE YEARS (Off-Broadway 2002)

Music and Lyrics by Jason Robert Brown

This two-person show chronicles the beginning, middle and deterioration of a relationship between a successful writer and a struggling actress. The show's form is unique. Cathy starts at the end of the relationship, and tells her story backwards, while Jamie starts at the beginning. The only point of intersection is the middle at their engagement. Jamie sings **"If I Didn't Believe in You"** while in an argument when Cathy refuses to go to a party being thrown by the publishers of his book.

THE LITTLE MERMAID (Broadway 2008)

Music by Alan Menken
Lyrics by Howard Ashman and Glenn Slater

Based on the Hans Christian Andersen tale, the 1989 animated Disney film *The Little Mermaid* was the basis for the stage musical, with several added songs. Ariel, a young, sea-dwelling mermaid, longs to be human. She falls in love with the human prince and, aided by some magic, gets her wish. **"Her Voice"** is one of the new songs added for the Broadway musical. Eric sings it after he is thrown overboard during a storm in Act I and saved by Ariel, who swims him safely to shore. Eric vows that he will find this woman (actually, a mermaid at that point) who saved his life, though he remembers only her voice and beautiful singing.

LITTLE WOMEN (Broadway 2005)
Music by Jason Howland
Lyrics by Mindi Dickstein

The musical is based on the famous 1869 American novel by Louisa May Alcott about the close-knit March family of Concord, Massachusetts, during and after the Civil War. Four sisters (Jo, Meg, Amy, and Beth) and their mother (Marmee) make the best they can of their lives while the patriarch of the household is serving in the U.S. Army as a chaplain. Laurie, a young man whose grandfather is against him having any relationship with the March family, expresses his hope for friendship with Jo in **"Take a Chance on Me."** He later proposes, and she declines, leaving him heartbroken. Jo, an aspiring writer, lands in New York. Laurie winds up marrying Jo's sister Amy. Jo matures as a young woman and a writer, and has a loving relationship with the older Professor Bhaer. The story ends with the announcement that Jo's book, *Little Women*, about her life with her sisters, has found a publisher.

NATASHA, PIERRE & THE GREAT COMET OF 1812 (Broadway 2016)
Music and Lyrics by Dave Malloy

The musical is based on part five of the second volume of Leo Tolstoy's *War and Peace*, set in Moscow of 1812. The countess Natasha Rostova is engaged to be married to Prince Andrey who is away fighting in the Napoleonic Wars. Near the beginning of the show, when Natasha and her cousin Sonya arrive in Moscow to stay with Marya D., Natasha's godmother. Natasha becomes involved in Moscow society and meets the charming and roguish Prince Anatole at the opera. They flirt, court, and decide to elope, despite the fact that Anatole is already married (though Natasha does not know this). Natasha breaks off her engagement with Prince Andrey. Her cousin Sonya discovers the plan and desperately attempts to convince Natasha that running away with Prince Anatole is misguided and will ruin her reputation irreparably. Soon, the Prince's marital status is brought to light and he is run out of town. Natasha attempts suicide, but survives. The other primary character of the story is Pierre, a philosophical drunk aristocrat discontent with his life. He attempts to stir compassion for Natasha in his best friend Andrey, who has returned from fighting, but Andrey will not marry Natasha. Natasha is comforted by the hope that her young life has myriad potential. After a night of drinking and an impromptu duel, Pierre considers his life choices in **"Dust and Ashes."** He determines to be more attentive to his life and future.

THOROUGHLY MODERN MILLIE (Broadway 2002)
Music by Jeanine Tesori
Lyrics by Dick Scanlan

Based on the 1967 movie starring Julie Andrews, *Thoroughly Modern Millie*, the stage musical retained only three of the songs from the movie (including the title song), with additional score. It chronicles the life of Millie, a transplanted Kansas girl trying to make it big in New York in the flapper days of 1922. Millie gets a job as a stenographer at the Sincere Trust Insurance Company. She intends to marry her wealthy boss, but falls for a charming but poor paper clip salesman, Jimmy Smith. **"What Do I Need with Love"** is Jimmy's song from Act I. After meeting Millie he realizes he has feelings for her, but finds them inconveniently out of step with his plan to play the field. In the end Millie, in love with Jimmy, finds out he is a rich millionaire posing as a pauper and they end up together.

THE UNAUTHORIZED AUTOBIOGRAPHY OF SAMANTHA BROWN
Music and Lyrics by Kait Kerrigan and Brian Lowdermilk

The songwriters' synopsis from *The Kerrigan-Lowdermilk Songbook*: "Samantha Brown is the valedictorian of her high school and up until this year, she's always had a clear path ahead of her. When her best friend is killed in a car accident, Sam starts to question everything that she knew about herself. Who is she now? When [best friend] Kelly dies, Sam feels like 'real life was the ghost.' Nothing moves her. Nothing wakes her up. Except one thing. She's at the DMV with [boyfriend] Adam, waiting to take her driver's test for the fourth time, when Adam offers a romantic escape from all her problems in **'Run Away With Me.'"** As of this writing the show has not had an Off-Broadway production.

DUST AND ASHES

from *Natasha, Pierre & The Great Comet of 1812*

Music and Lyrics by
Dave Malloy
Based on *War and Peace* by Leo Tolstoy

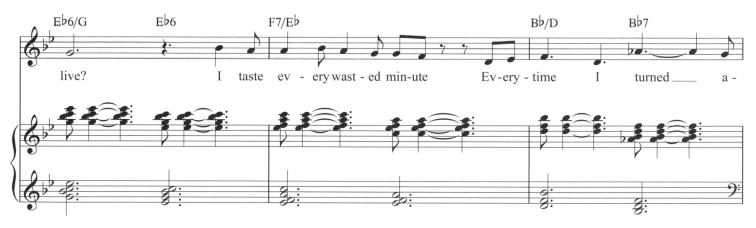

live? I taste ev - ery wast - ed min-ute Ev-ery - time I turned ___ a -

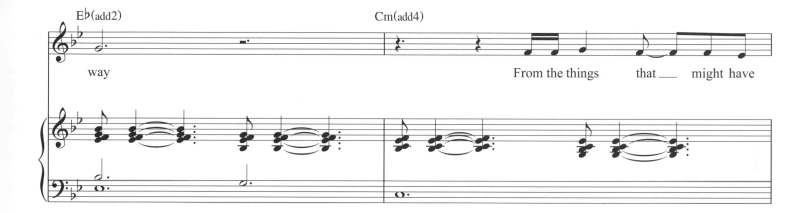

way From the things that ___ might have

healed me How long have I been sleep-ing Is this how I

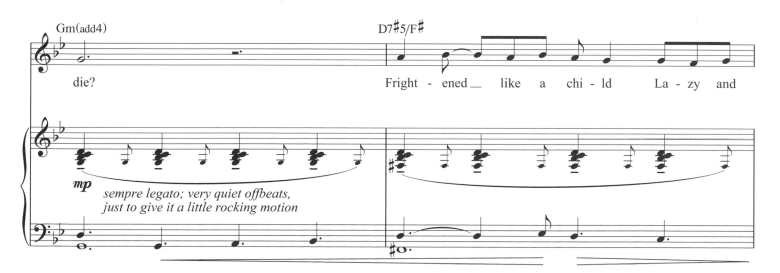

die? Fright - ened ___ like a chi - ld La - zy and

*sempre legato; very quiet offbeats,
just to give it a little rocking motion*

numb · · · Is this how I die? _____ Pre-

tend - ing __ and pre-pos-ter-ous __ and dumb

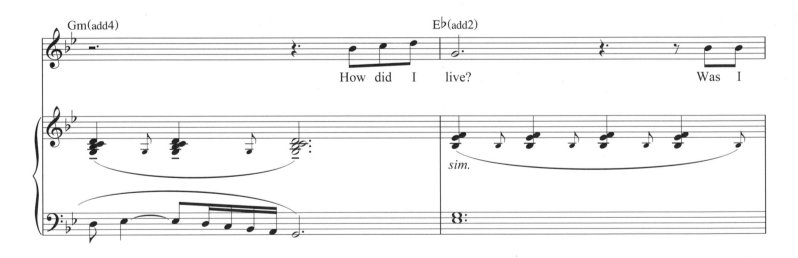

How did I live? Was I

kind e-nough and good e-nough? Did I love _____ e

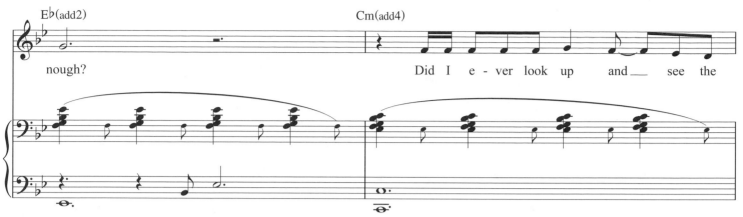

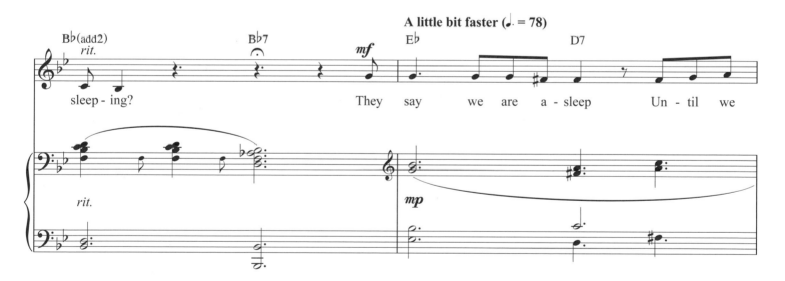

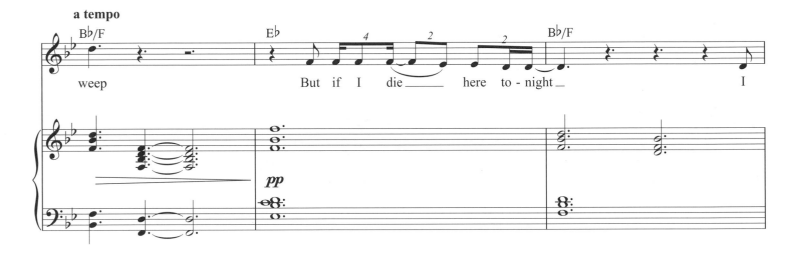

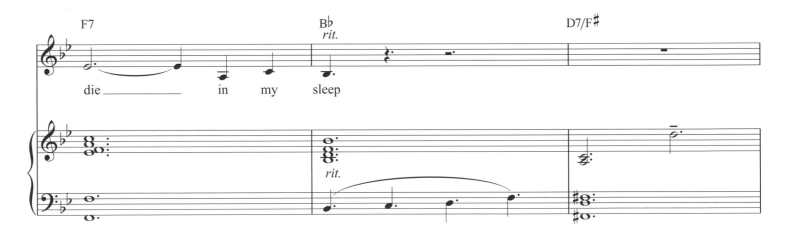

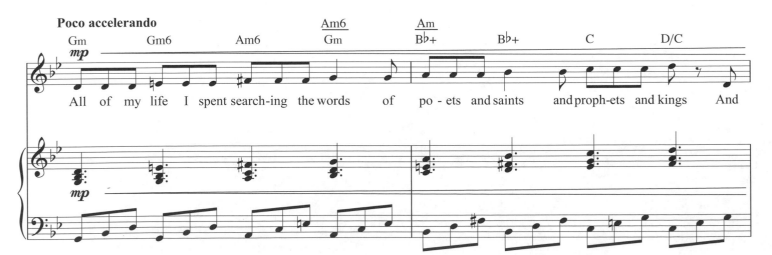

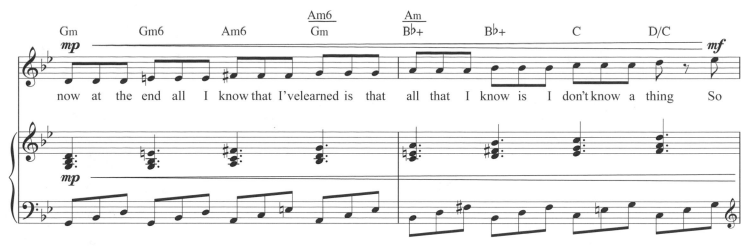

now at the end all I know that I've learned is that all that I know is I don't know a thing So

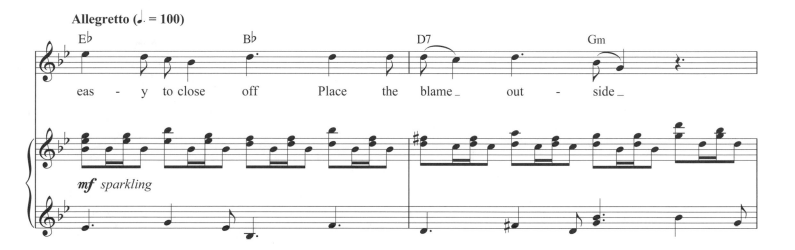

Allegretto (♩. = 100)

eas - y to close off Place the blame out - side

Hid - ing in my room at night so terr - i - fied

all the things I could have been but I nev - er had the nerve

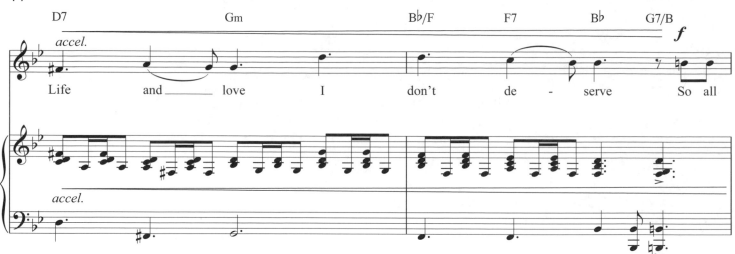

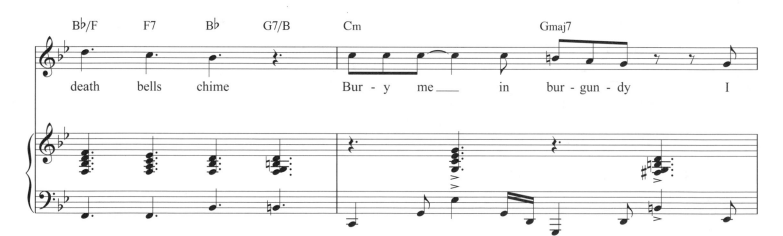

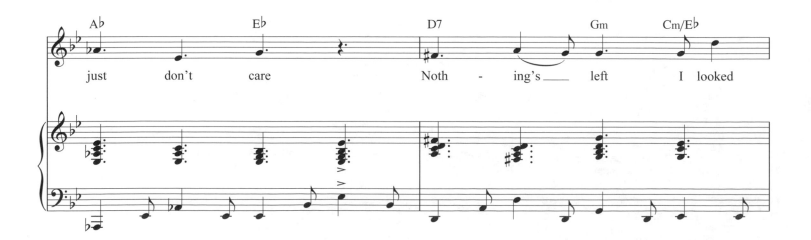

Raucous; a la New Orleans funeral march

ev - ery - where Is this how I die? Was there

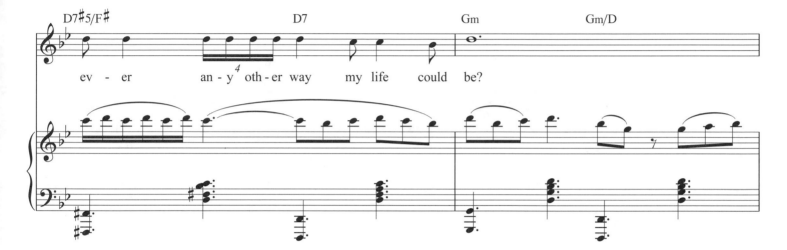

ev - er an - y oth-er way my life could be?

Is this how I die? _____ Such a

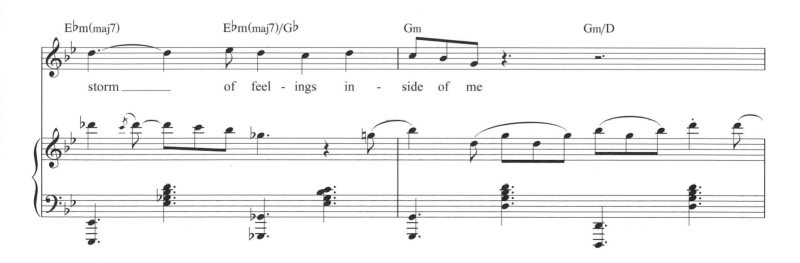

storm _____ of feel - ings in - side of me

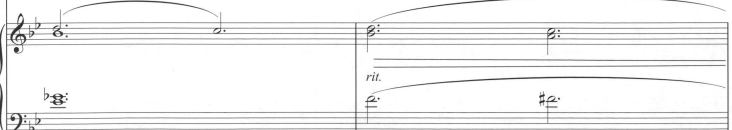

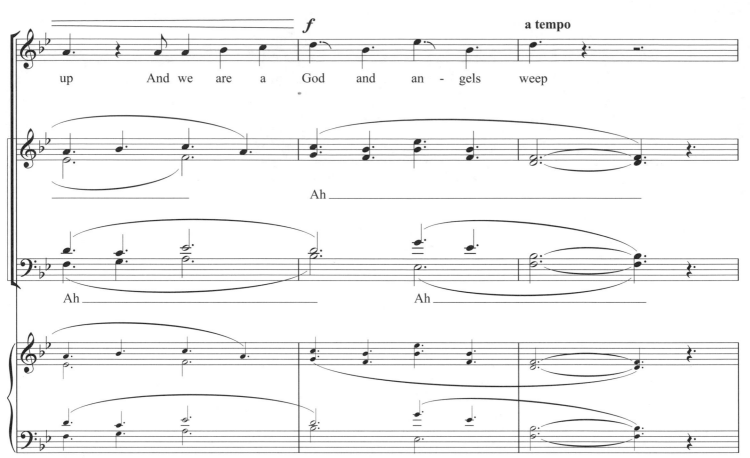

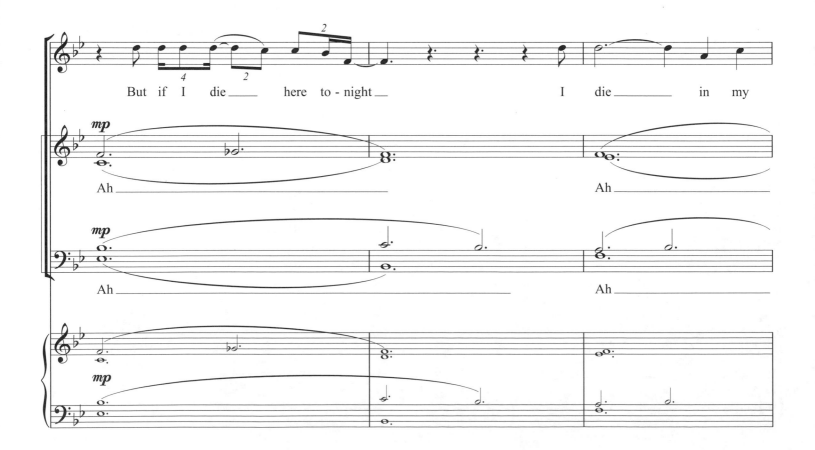

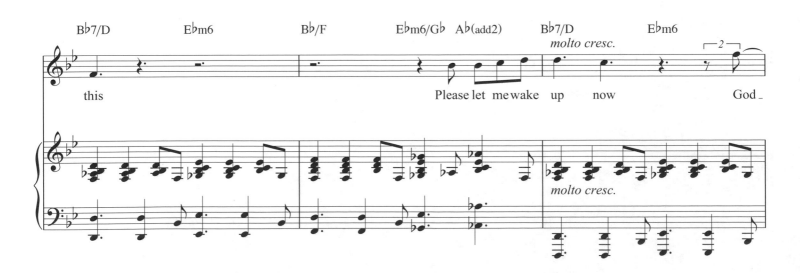

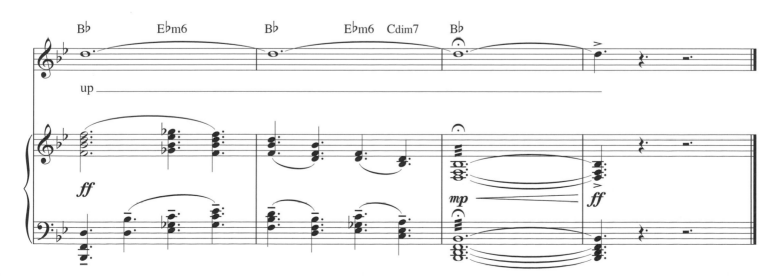

DUST AND ASHES

from *Natasha, Pierre & The Great Comet of 1812*

audition excerpt

Music and Lyrics by
Dave Malloy
Based on *War and Peace* by Leo Tolstoy

So all right, all right, I've had my ___ time

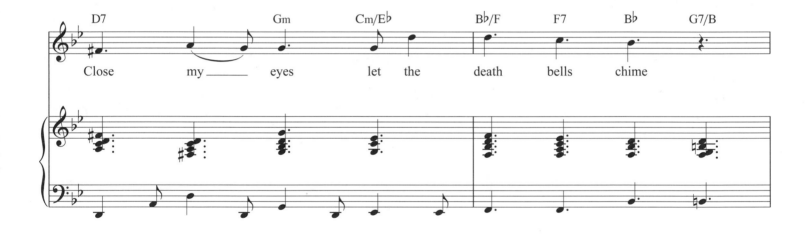

Close my ___ eyes let the death bells chime

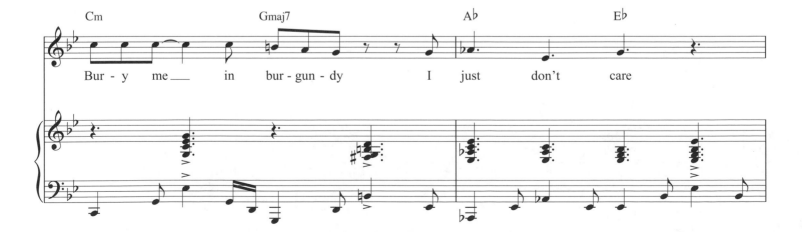

Bur - y me ___ in bur-gun-dy I just don't care

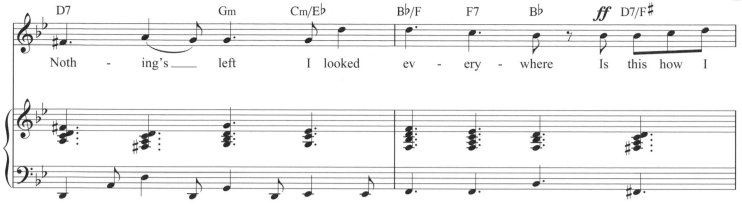

Noth - ing's___ left I looked ev - ery - where Is this how I

Raucous; a la New Orleans funeral march

die? Was there ev - er an - y oth - er way my life could

be? Is this how I

die?_____ Such a storm___ of feel - ings in - side of me

FIGHT THE DRAGONS

from *Big Fish*

Music and Lyrics by
Andrew Lippa

make a friend, __ and pray the day__ will nev - er end,___ 'cuz there's one more ad - ven-

- ture wait - in' 'round___ an - oth - er bend_____ where I fight the __ drag -

mf as before

Pedal okay

- ons and I storm the__ cas - tles and I win a__ bat -

- tle or __ two._____ But then a feel - ing__ comes,__

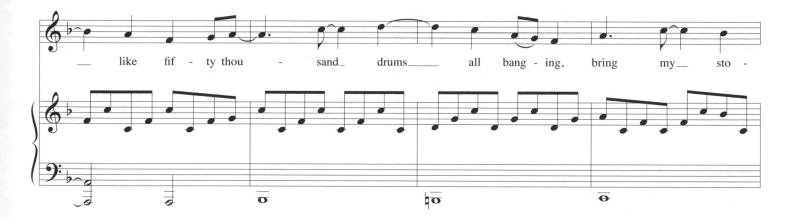

like fif - ty thou - sand drums___ all bang - ing, bring my__ sto -

ries home___ to you. And I won - der as I wan-

-der on the road___ from door to door,___ ex - act - ly what you think__

___ of where I've been.___ Do you know___ I joined the cir -

- cus, met a mer - maid, __ fought a war? __ Do you know I think of you __

__ through thick and thin? __ Be - cause e - ven though __ I'm

mak - ing deals __ and bring - in' peo - ple joy, __ I'm u - sually on - ly

rit. **Slower**

think - ing of __ my boy. Out there on the road __ I pray __

Freely   **Tempo I**

tell - ing sto - ries to your son.   Then we

Aggressive, accented

fight the__ drag - ons and then storm the__ cast - les and I

do the__ best_____ that I____ can._____   But ev - 'ry-bod-

- y__ knows____ that's how the sto - ry__ goes_____ to turn__ each

Pedal okay

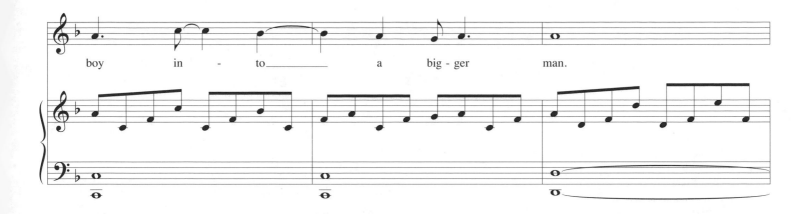

boy in - to_____ a big - ger man.

rit.

So I'll fight the___ drag -

ons_____ 'til___ you can._____

rit.

FIGHT THE DRAGONS

from *Big Fish*

audition excerpt

Music and Lyrics by
Andrew Lippa

can._____ But ev-'ry-bod _ _ y____ knows____

_____ that's how the sto - ry____ goes_____ to turn___ each

boy in - to_____ a big - ger man.

dim.

mf

Pedal okay

HER VOICE
from *The Little Mermaid - A Broadway Musical*

Music by Alan Menken
Lyrics by Glenn Slater

Some-where there's a girl who's like the shim-mer of the wind up-on the

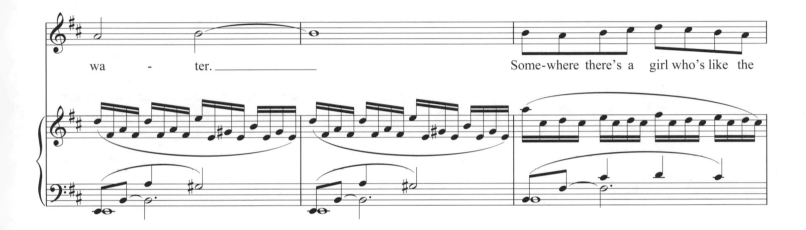

wa - ter._____ Some-where there's a girl who's like the

glim-mer of the sun-light on the sea._____

Some-where there's a girl who's like a swell of end - less mu - sic.____

And that sound, it haunts my dreams and spins me 'round un-til it seems I'm fly-ing,

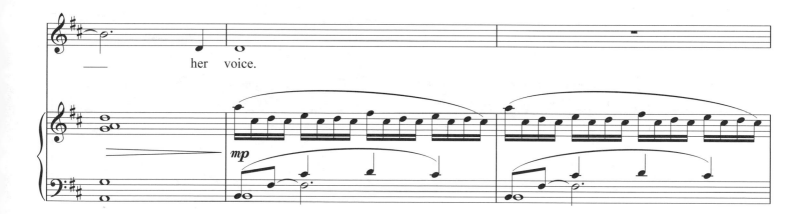

her voice.

I can sense her laugh-ter in the

rip - ple of the waves a - gainst the shore - line.

I can see her smil - ing in the moon - light as it set - tles on the sand.

I can feel her wait - ing just be - yond the pale ho -

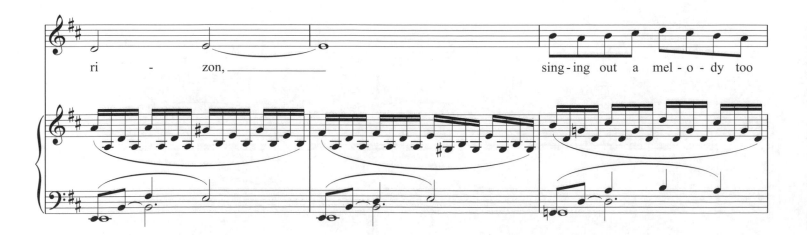

ri - zon, sing - ing out a mel - o - dy too

love - ly to with - stand. _____ And her

molto rall.

a tempo

voice, it's there as dusk is fall - ing. _____

f a tempo

_____ And her voice, it's there as dawn steals

by. _____ Pure and bright, it's

al - ways near. All day, all night, and still I hear it

call - ing, _____ her

rit.

Più mosso

voice. _____

rit.

mp

Meno mosso, poco rubato

Strange as a dream,

Real as the sea. If you can hear me now, ___ come set me free, ___

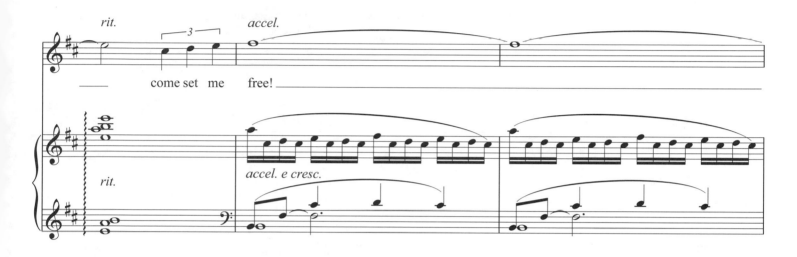

___ come set me free! ___

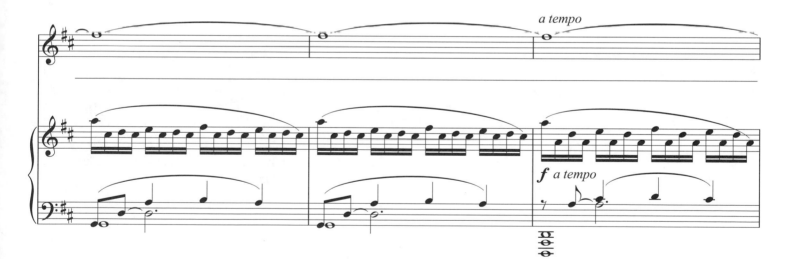

HER VOICE

from *The Little Mermaid - A Broadway Musical*

audition excerpt

Music by Alan Menken
Lyrics by Glenn Slater

bright,   it's al - ways near.   All

day,   all   night,   and   still   I   hear   it   call   -   ing, _____

her   voice

I AM ALDOLPHO

from *The Drowsy Chaperone*

Words and Music by Lisa Lambert
and Greg Morrison

dol-pho. Well, love-ly miss I am the same Al-dol - pho. I in-tro-

duce my-self, I am Al-dol-pho. Not so fast... So

just in case you did-n't hear Al-dol-pho, I'll try to make it ver-y clear: Al-

dol-pho. The love-ly lad-ies al-ways cheer Al-dol - pho when I re-

peat my-self, I am Al - dol-pho. I can sing it high: Al-dol-pho.

colla voce

Freely

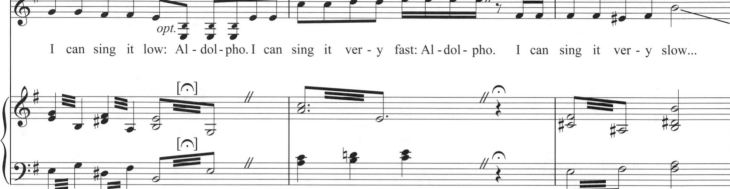

I can sing it low: Al-dol-pho. I can sing it ver-y fast: Al-dol-pho. I can sing it ver-y slow...

ly *I'd do it now, but it would take hours. Now let us see if you can remember my name.* Now who's the fel-low that you see? Al-

dol-pho. And how should you re-fer to me? Al-dol-pho. And who is it I'll al-ways be? Al-

dol-pho.   Now sing it proud-ly   I am Al-dol - pho.   Now let me spell it out for

you   *for all you lovely ladies who didn't hear,*
for some reason maybe you are hard of
hearing or something - I don't know. It goes
a - a - a - a - a - al

[*colla voce*]

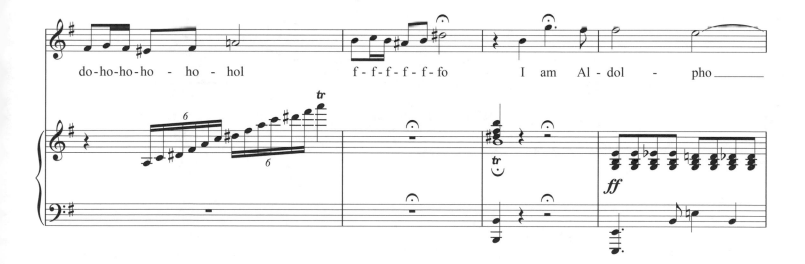

do-ho-ho-ho - ho-hol   f - f - f - f - f-fo   I am Al-dol - pho _____

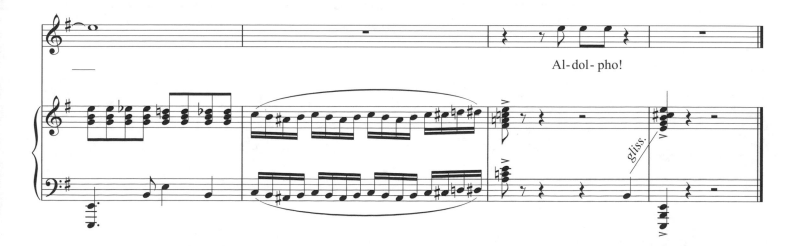

_____   Al-dol- pho!

gliss.

I AM ALDOLPHO

from *The Drowsy Chaperone*

audition excerpt

Words and Music by Lisa Lambert
and Greg Morrison

ALDOLPHO:

Now who's the fel - low that you see? Al - dol - pho. And how should you re - fer to me? Al - dol - pho. And who is it I'll al - ways be? Al -

dol - pho. Now sing it proud - ly I am Al - dol - pho.

Now let me spell it out for you a - a - a - a - a - al

do - ho - ho - ho - ho - ho - hol f - f - f - f - f - f - fo I am Al -

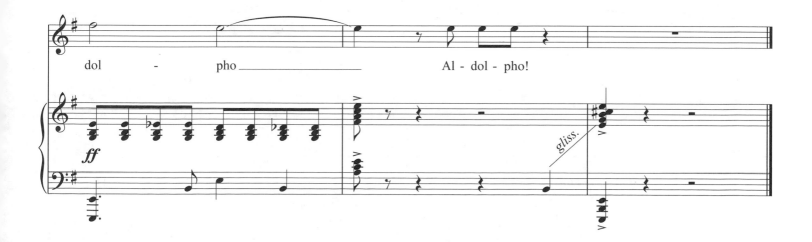

dol - pho _____ Al - dol - pho!

I BELIEVE
from the Broadway Musical *The Book of Mormon*

Words and Music by Trey Parker,
Robert Lopez and Matt Stone
Vocal Arrangement by Stephen Oremus

Chorus parts have been omitted from this solo voice edition.

Broadly

trust that my Lord is might - i - er, and al - ways has my back. Now I

Steady pop, in 4 (♩ = 82)

cresc. poco a poco

must be com - plete - ly de - vout. I can't have e - ven one shred of

doubt! I be - lieve ___ that the

Lord God cre - at - ed the u - ni - verse. I be - lieve ___ that he sent his on - ly Son to die ___

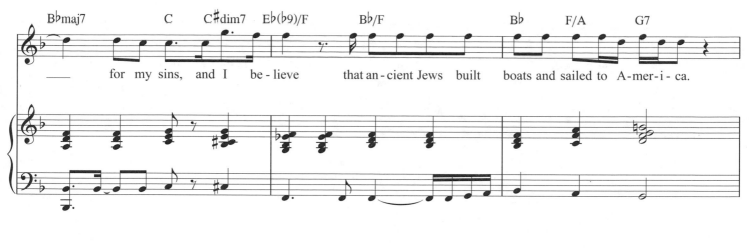

for my sins, and I be-lieve that an-cient Jews built boats and sailed to A-mer-i-ca.

I am a Mor-mon, and a Mor-mon just be-

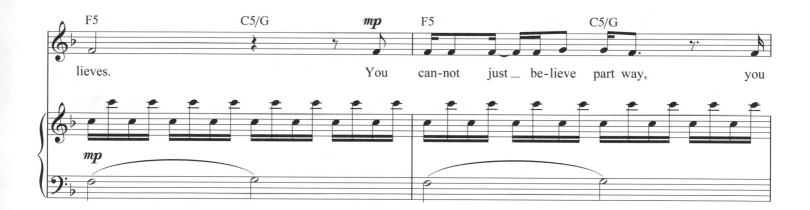

lieves. You can-not just be-lieve part way, you

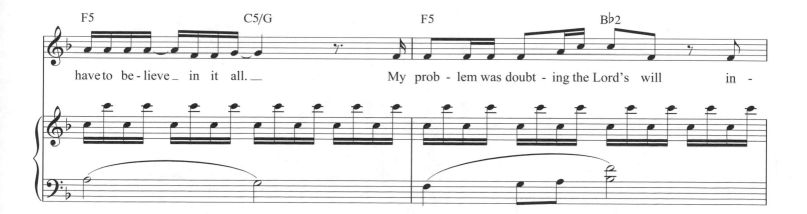

have to be-lieve in it all. My prob-lem was doubt-ing the Lord's will in-

stead of stand-ing tall. I can't al - low my-self to have an - y doubt. _ It's time to

set my wor - ries free. _ Time to show the world what El - der Price is a - bout, and

share the pow-er in - side of me! I be - lieve _____ that

God has a plan for all __ of us. I be - lieve __ that plan in - volves

me get-ting my own plan-et. And I be - lieve that the cur-rent pres-i-dent of the church, Thom-as

Mon - son, speaks di - rect-ly to God. _ I am a Mor - mon, and,

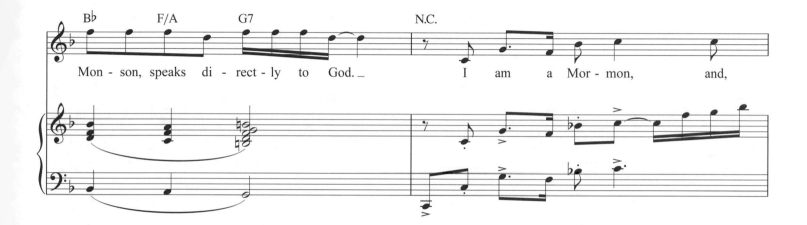

dang it, a Mor - mon just be - lieves. I

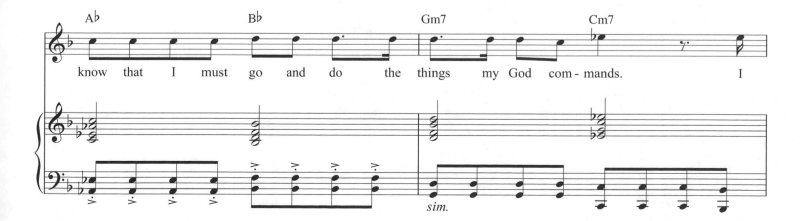

know that I must go and do the things my God com - mands. I

God has sent __ me here. And I be-lieve that in nine-teen sev-en-ty-eight God

changed his mind __ a-bout black peo-ple. __ You can be a Mor-mon,

a Mor-mon who just be-lieves. And

now I can feel __ the ex-cite-ment. This is the mo-ment I was born to do. __ And I

feel so in-cred-i-ble to be shar-ing my faith with you. The

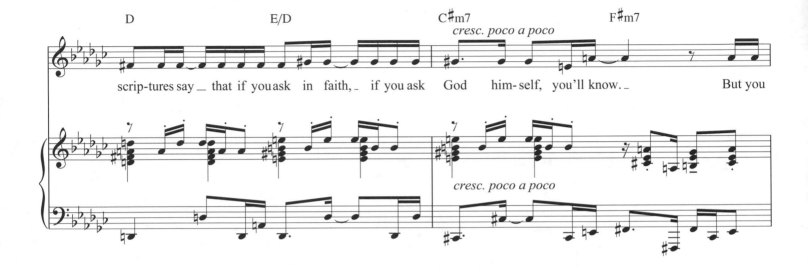

scrip-tures say that if you ask in faith, if you ask God him-self, you'll know. But you

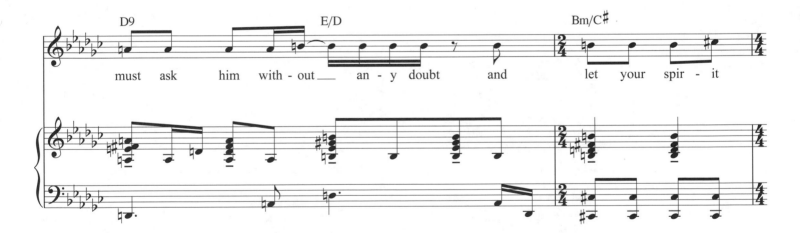

must ask him with-out an-y doubt and let your spir-it

grow. I be-lieve that

God lives on a plan-et called Ko-lob. I be-lieve ___ that Je - sus has

his own plan-et as well. And I be - lieve that the Gar - den of E - den was in

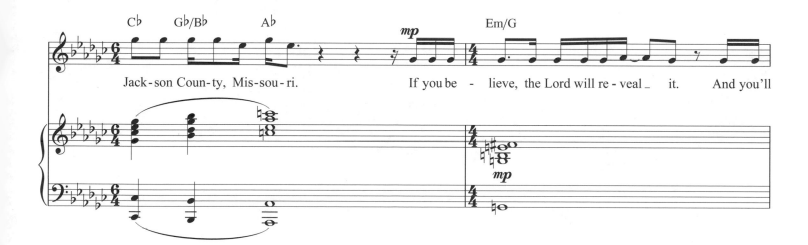

Jack-son Coun-ty, Mis-sou-ri. If you be - lieve, the Lord will re - veal ___ it. And you'll

know it's all true, ___ you'll just feel it. You'll be a Mor - mon, and,

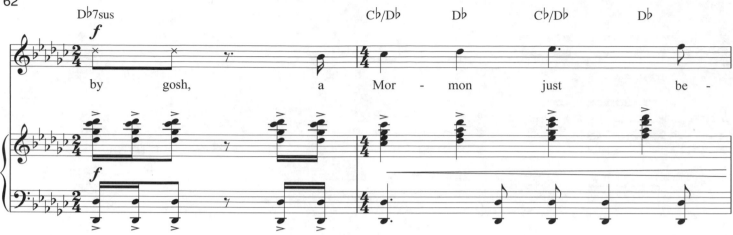

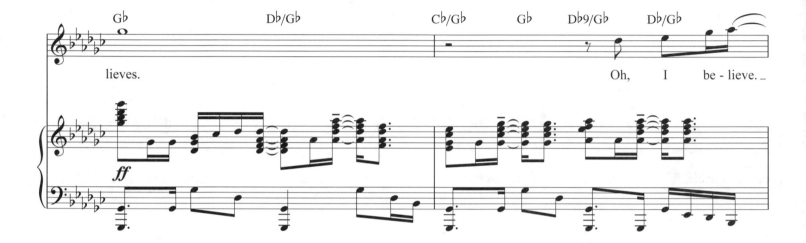

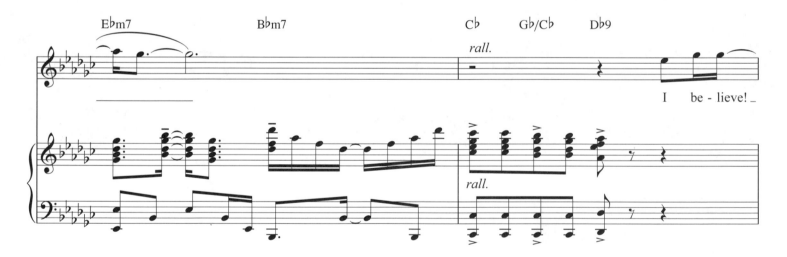

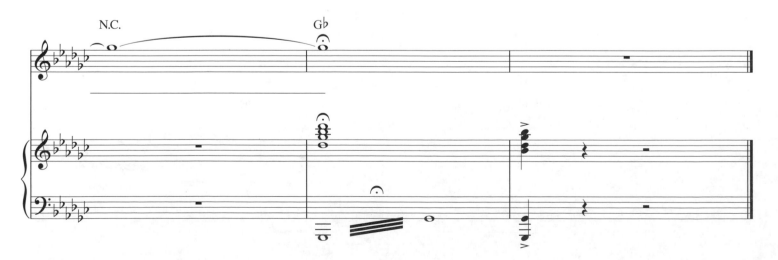

I BELIEVE

from the Broadway Musical *The Book of Mormon*

audition excerpt

Words and Music by Trey Parker,
Robert Lopez and Matt Stone
Vocal Arrangement by Stephen Oremus

This page has been left blank to facilitate page turns.

IF I DIDN'T BELIEVE IN YOU

from *The Last Five Years*

Music and Lyrics by
Jason Robert Brown

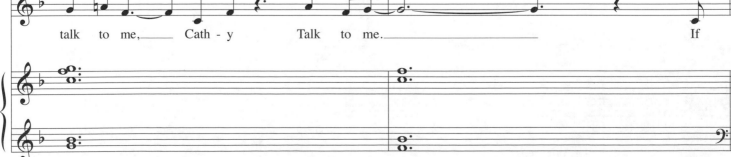

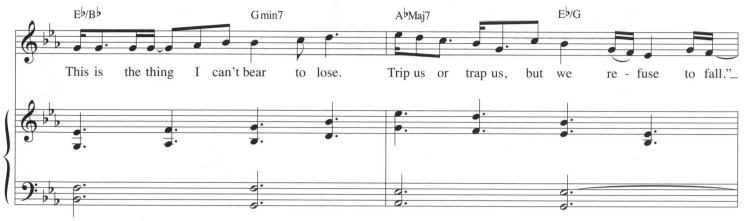

This is the thing I can't bear to lose. Trip us or trap us, but we re - fuse to fall."

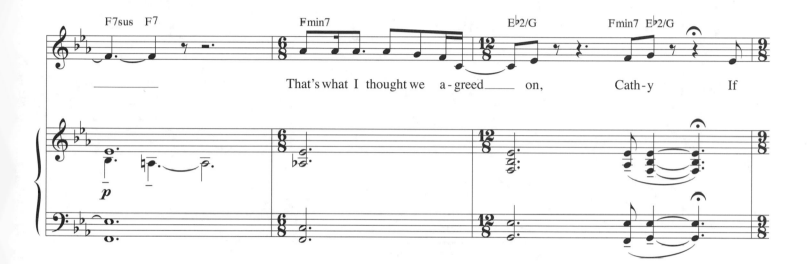

_____ That's what I thought we a - greed _____ on, Cath - y If

I had-n't be-lieved in ___ you, I would-n't have loved you ___ at all. ___

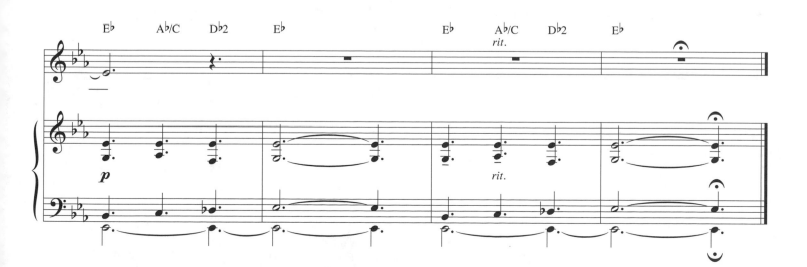

IF I DIDN'T BELIEVE IN YOU

from *The Last Five Years*

audition excerpt

Music and Lyrics by
Jason Robert Brown

fine! Just hang on and you'll

see! But don't make me

wait 'til you do To be hap - py with you Will you

lis - ten to me?

PROUD OF YOUR BOY

from *Aladdin*

Music by Alan Menken
Lyrics by Howard Ashman

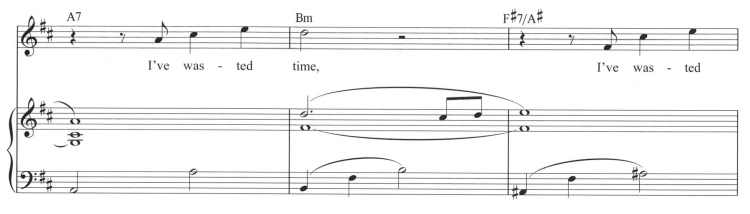

I've was - ted time, I've was - ted

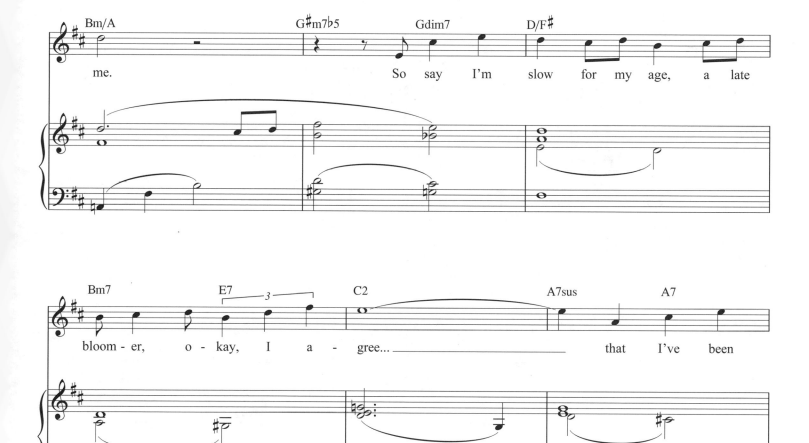

me. So say I'm slow for my age, a late

bloom - er, o - kay, I a - gree... that I've been

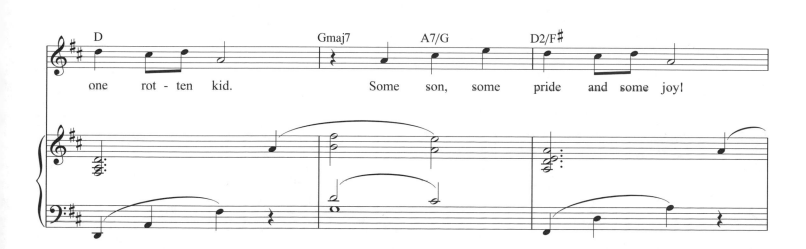

one rot - ten kid. Some son, some pride and some joy!

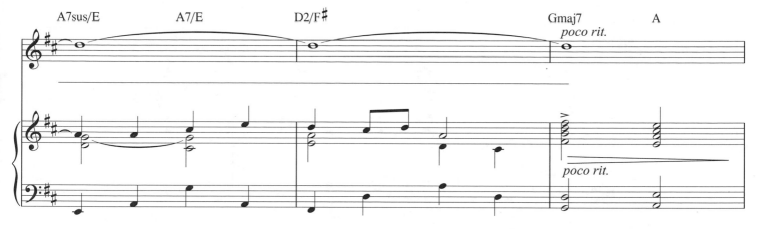

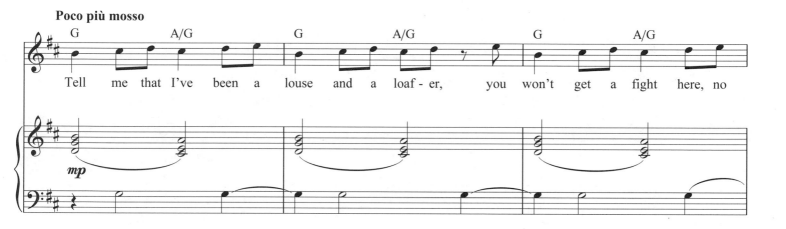

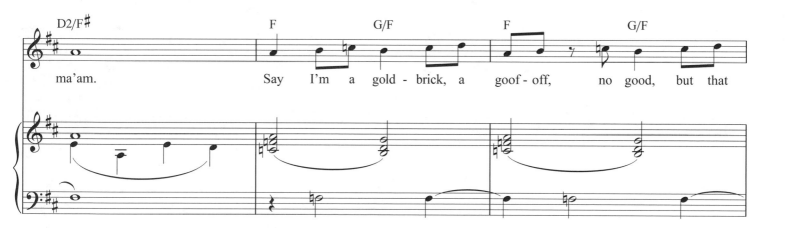

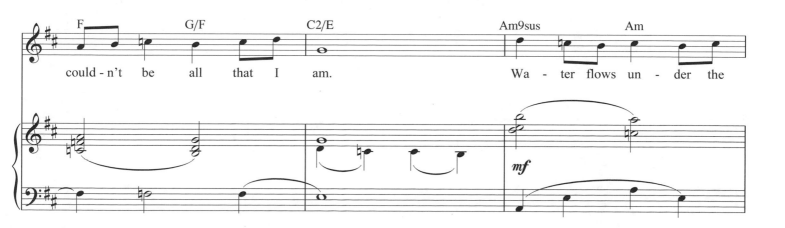

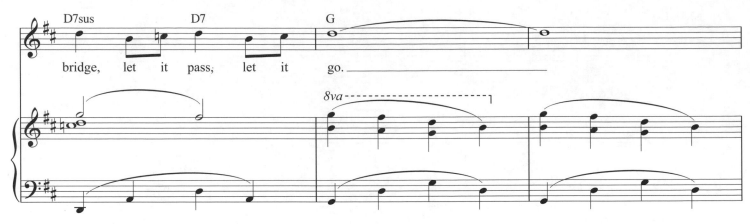

bridge, let it pass; let it go._____

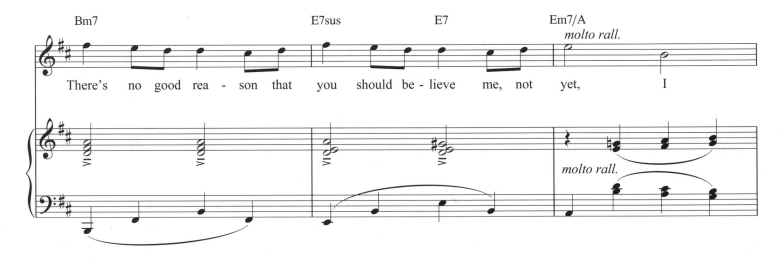

There's no good rea - son that you should be - lieve me, not yet, I

A tempo, grandly

know, but... Some - day and soon, I'll make you

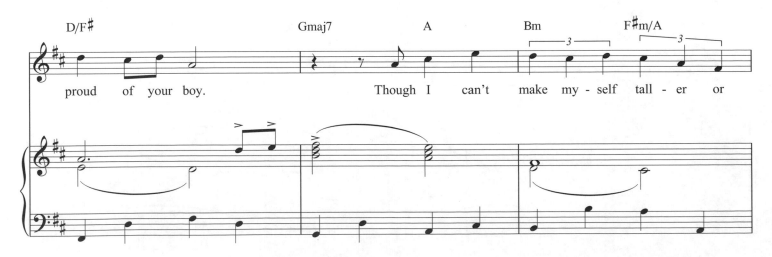

proud of your boy. Though I can't make my - self tall - er or

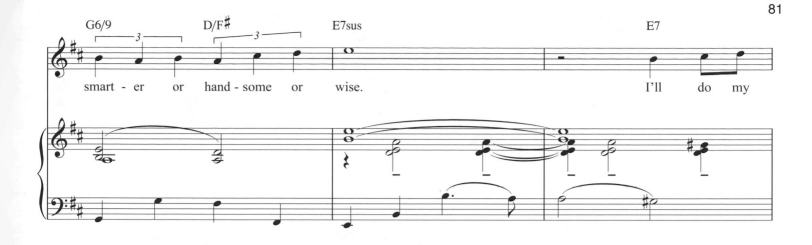

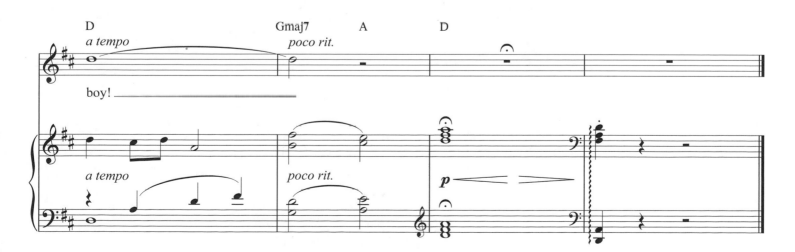

PROUD OF YOUR BOY

from *Aladdin*

audition excerpt

Music by Alan Menken
Lyrics by Howard Ashman

RIGHT BEFORE MY EYES

from *Ever After*

Lyrics by Marcy Heisler
Music by Zina Goldrich

Why, in fact, is ev-'ry-bod-y here? What is right and wrong? Then you came a-long and

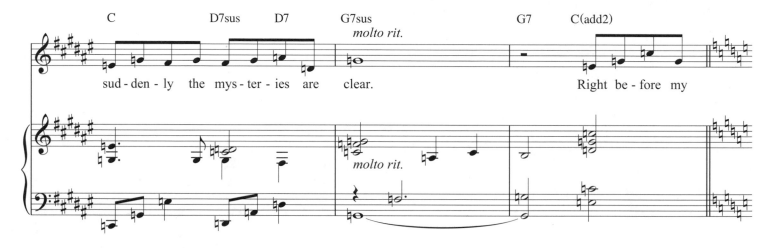

sud - den - ly the mys - ter - ies are clear. Right be - fore my

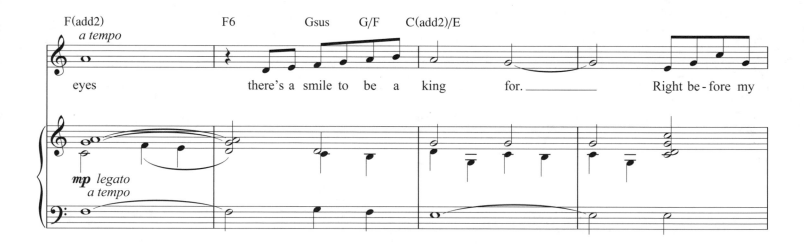

eyes there's a smile to be a king for. _____ Right be - fore my

eyes _____ there's a girl I long to know. There's a heart I long to

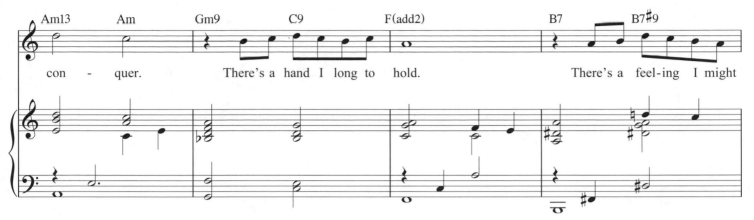

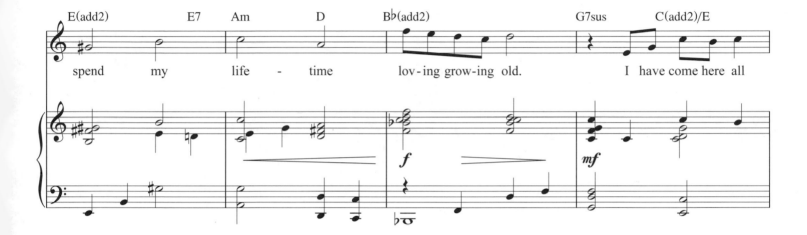

lis - ten - ing, in - deed. All the an - swers that I need are

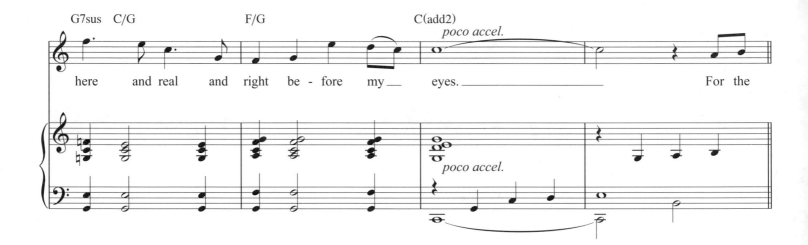

here and real and right be - fore my __ eyes. _____ For the

poco accel.

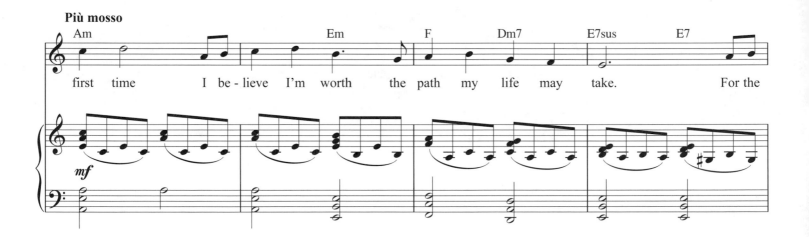

Più mosso

first time I be - lieve I'm worth the path my life may take. For the

first time I be - lieve that one can dream while wide a - wake. For the

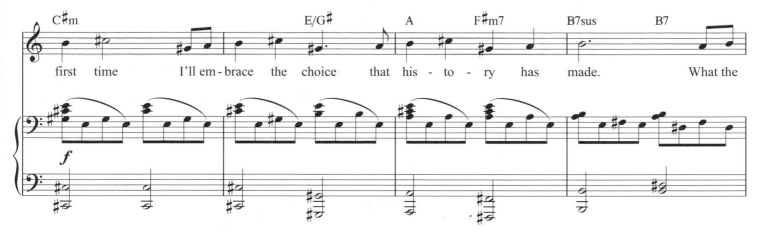

first time I'll em-brace the choice that his-to-ry has made. What the

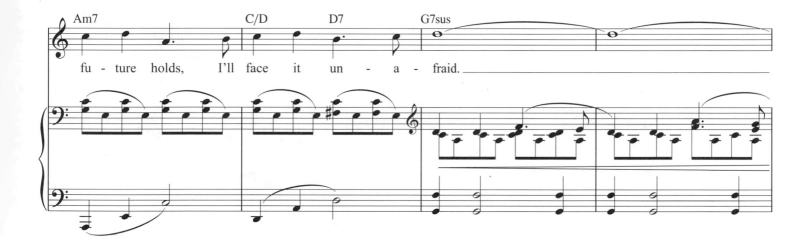

fu-ture holds, I'll face it un-a-fraid.

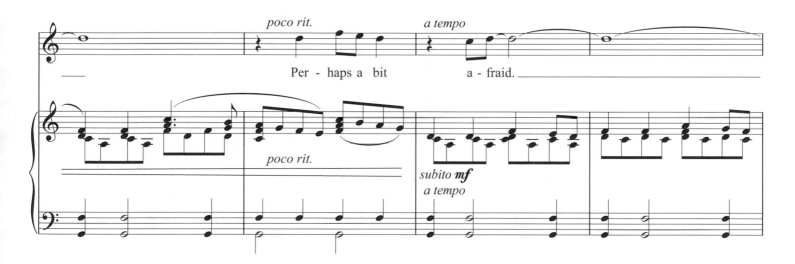

Per-haps a bit a-fraid.

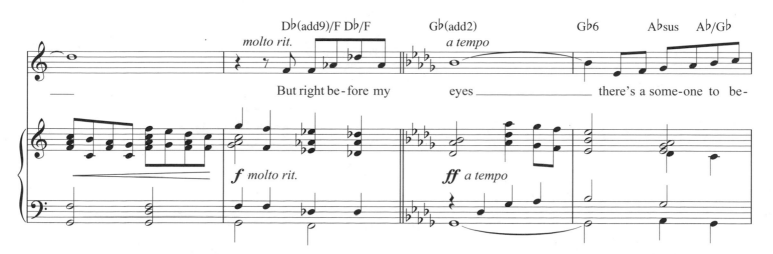

But right be-fore my eyes there's a some-one to be-

88

ques - tions. Now the an - swers come, but on - ly one ap -

plies. Fate was lis - ten - ing a - bove for I

found it in the love that's here and real and right be - fore my

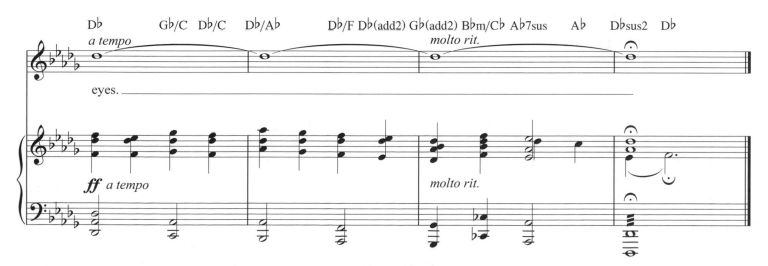

eyes.

RIGHT BEFORE MY EYES

from *Ever After*

audition excerpt

Lyrics by Marcy Heisler
Music by Zina Goldrich

This page has been left blank to facilitate page turns.

RUN AWAY WITH ME

from *The Unauthorized Autobiography of Samantha Brown*

Words and Music by
Kait Kerrigan
and Brian Lowdermilk

Steady, in 1 (♩. = 60)

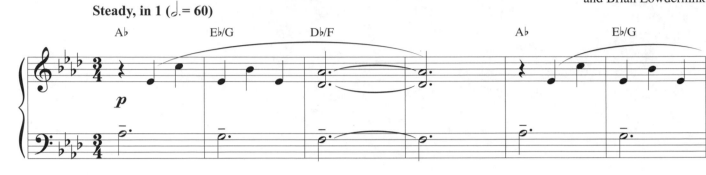

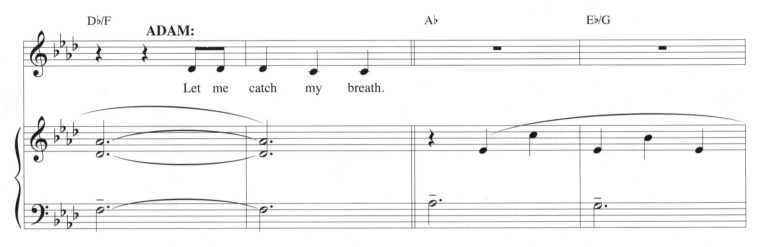

ADAM: Let me catch my breath.

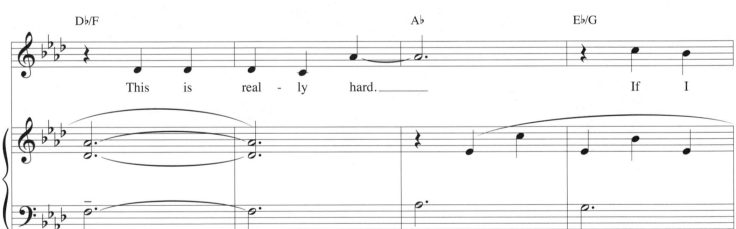

This is real - ly hard._____ If I

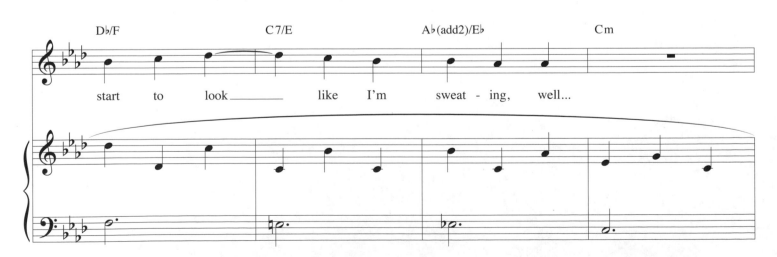

start to look_____ like I'm sweat - ing, well...

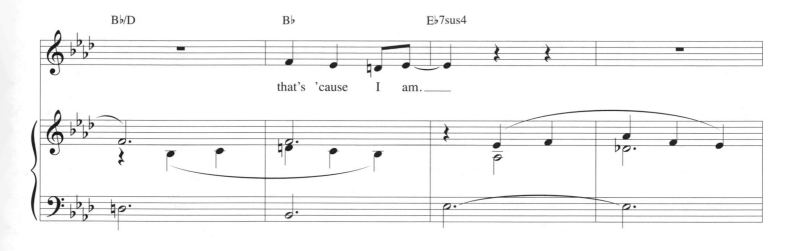

that's 'cause I am.____

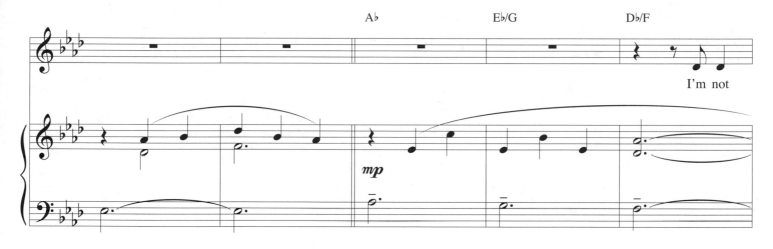

I'm not

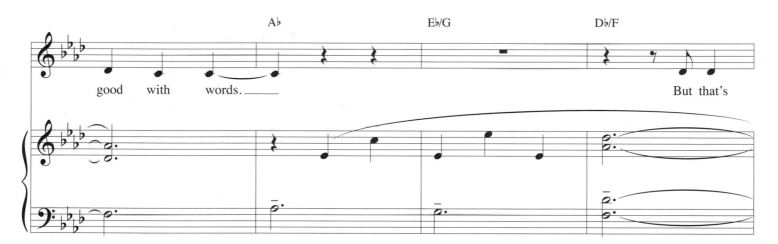

good with words.____ But that's

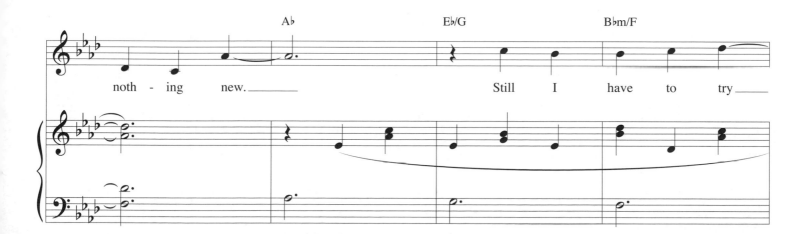

noth - ing new.____ Still I have to try____

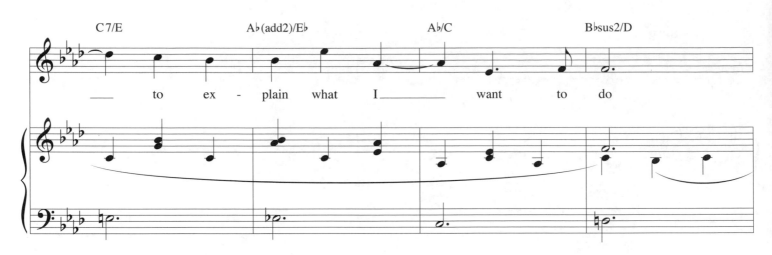

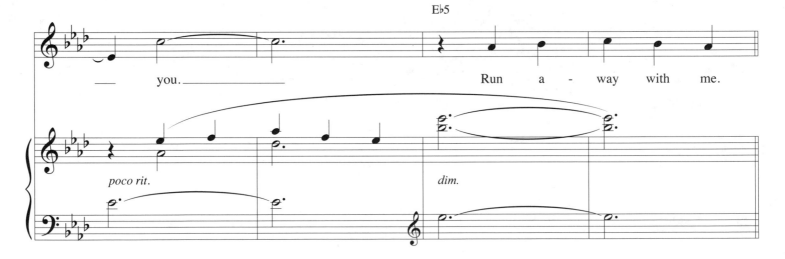

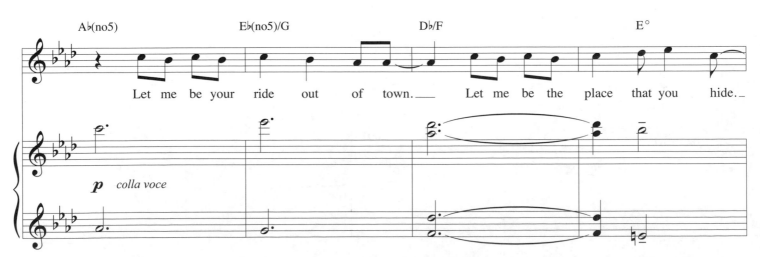

Fm9

F7

-where._____ Get the car__

with pedal

Bbm7

Ebsus4

___ packed and throw__ me the key.__ Run a - way with me.__

Ab

Eb/G

Db(add2)

_____ Sam, I know it's fast.__
I know this is fast.__

mp *lush, thick*

Ab

Cm7/G

Dbmaj7/F

I'm in love with you.__
What else can I do?__

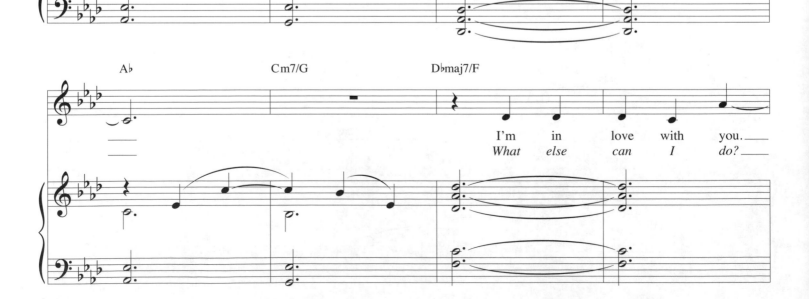

Let me be your ride out of town.___ Let me be the place that you hide.___

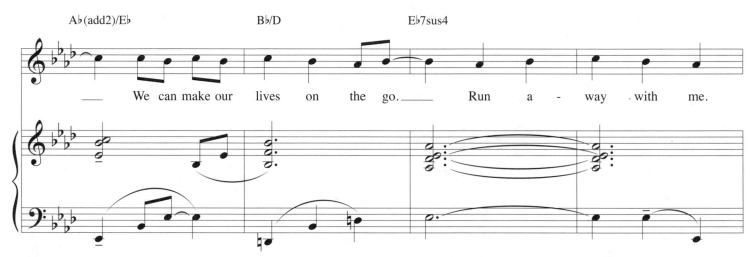

___ We can make our lives on the go.___ Run a - way with me.

Al - a - bam - a heat, sign me up!___ We'll be on the road like some

coun - try song. Won't be long.___ Sam, you're read - y. Let's___
We'll be read - y.

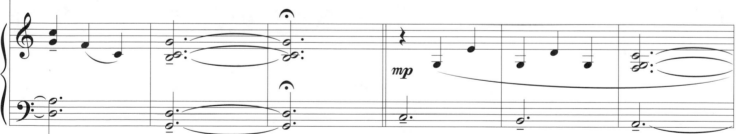

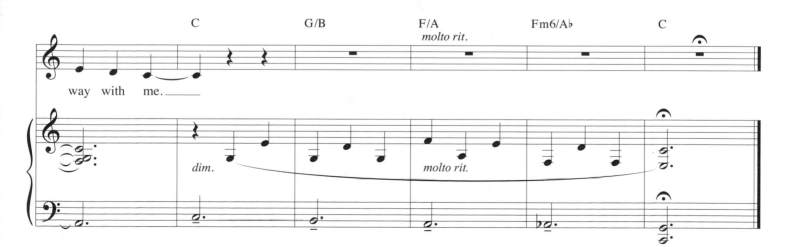

RUN AWAY WITH ME

from *The Unauthorized Autobiography of Samantha Brown*

audition excerpt

Words and Music by
Kait Kerrigan
and Brian Lowdermilk

Steady, in 1 (♩. = 60)

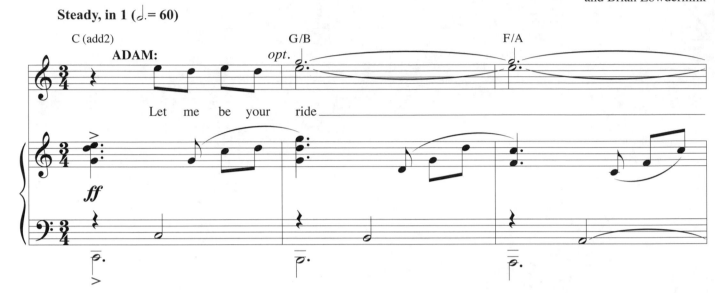

Let me be your ride

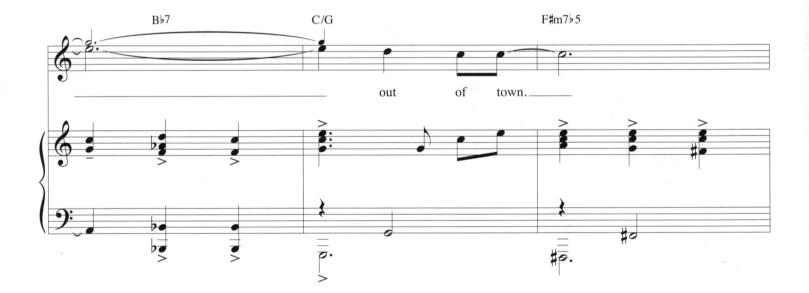

out of town.

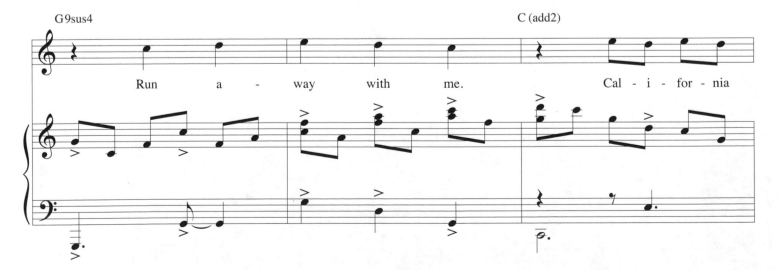

Run a - way with me. Cal - i - for - nia

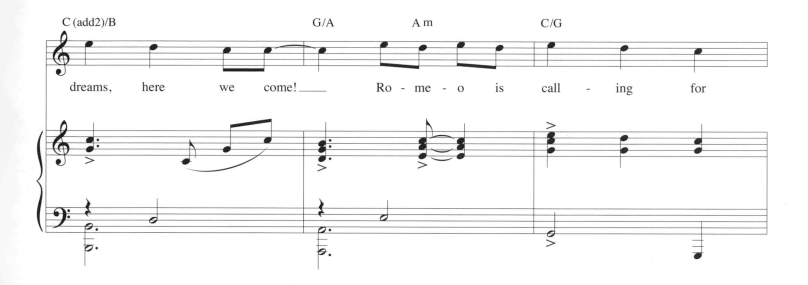

C (add2)/B — G/A — A m — C/G

dreams, here we come!___ Ro - me - o is call - ing for

F — E/F♯ — F/G

Ju - li - et. Read - y, set, Sam, you're
now you're

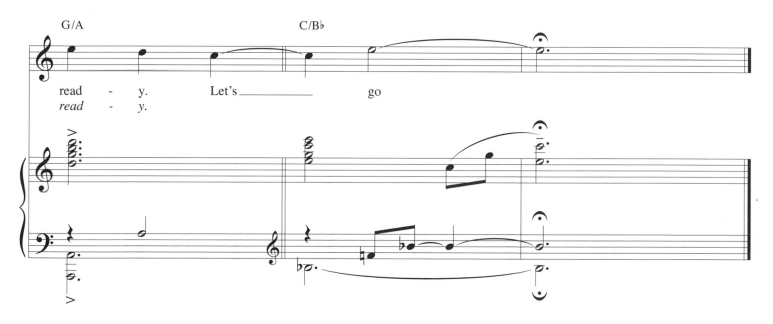

G/A — C/B♭

read - y. Let's_____ go
read - y.

This page has been left blank to facilitate page turns.

SIBELLA
from *A Gentleman's Guide to Love & Murder*

Music by Steven Lutvak
Lyrics by Robert L. Freedman and
Steven Lutvak

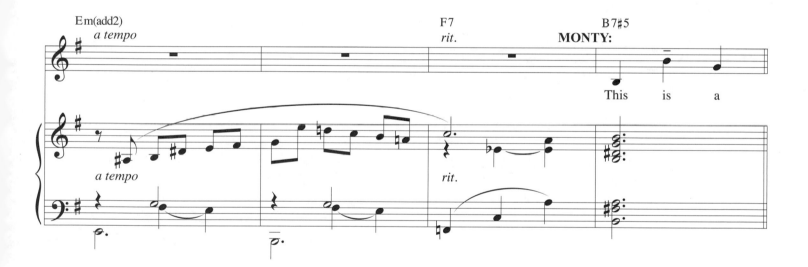

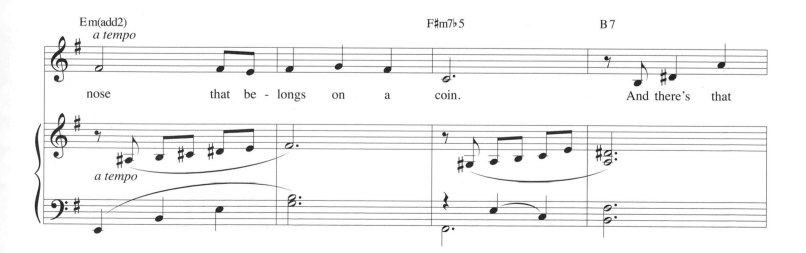

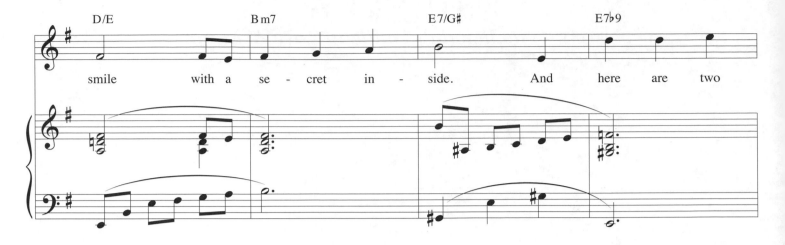

smile with a se - cret in - side. And here are two

eyes that are bright with a mis - chie - vous light you

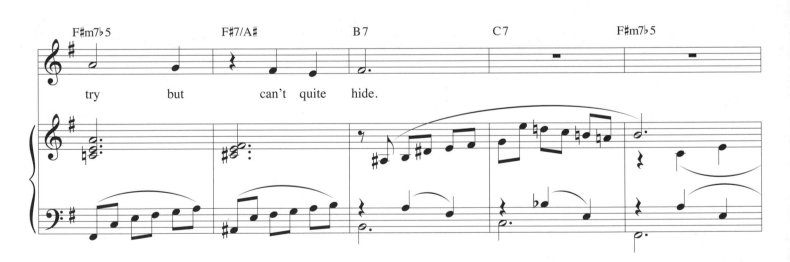

try but can't quite hide.

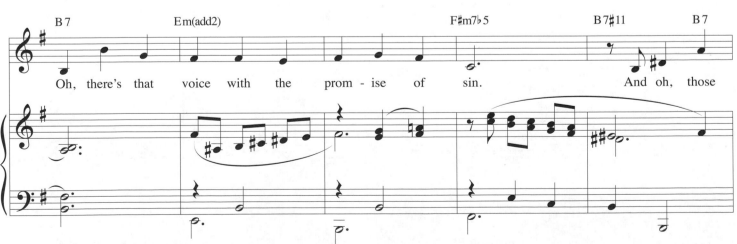

Oh, there's that voice with the prom - ise of sin. And oh, those

Em   E7/G♯   E7

lips   are   a   prom - ise   of   bliss,   and   I   know   that

Am(add2)   Cm6/E♭   Gsus/D   C♯m7♭5

your   em - brace   is   a   treach - er - ous   place.   There's

F♯m7♭5   Bsus   B+   Edim

dan - ger   in   your   kiss.   This   is   the

Moving forward

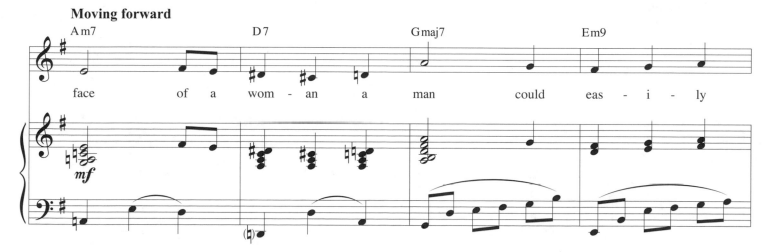

Am7   D7   Gmaj7   Em9

face   of   a   wom - an   a   man   could   eas - i - ly

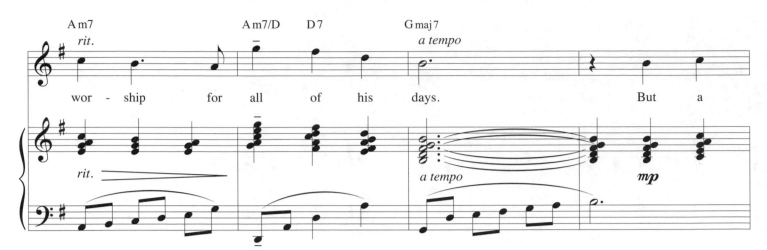

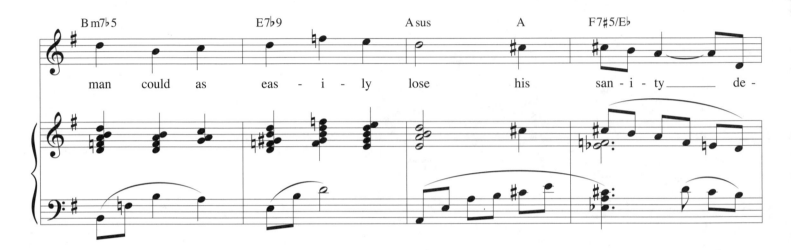

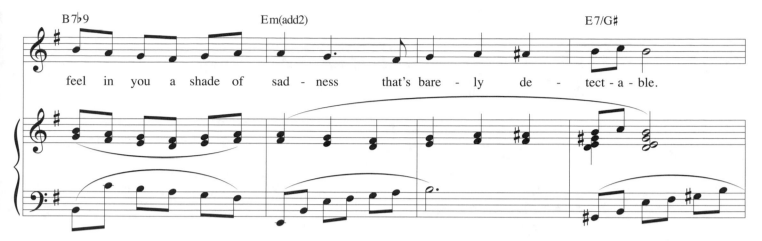

feel in you a shade of sad - ness that's bare - ly de - tect - a - ble.

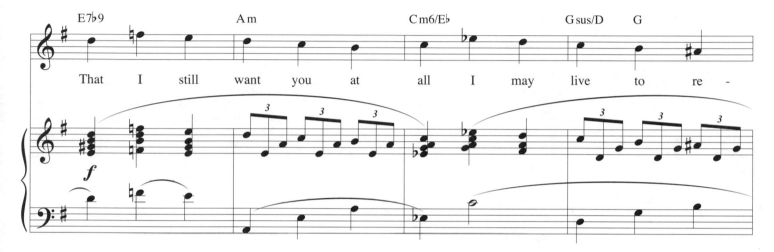

That I still want you at all I may live to re -

gret. You're de - ceit - ful. You're de - lect - a - ble.

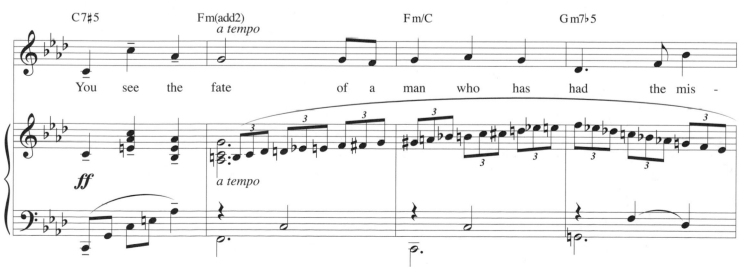

You see the fate of a man who has had the mis -

for - tune to spend his life caught in your sway.

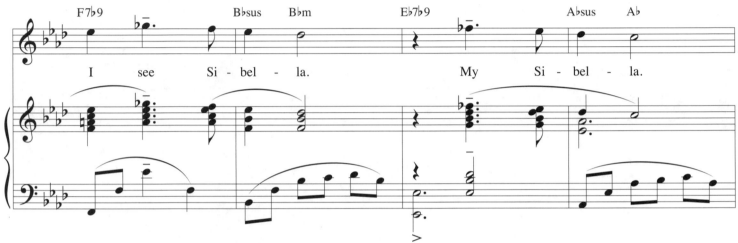

I see Si - bel - la. My Si - bel - la.

And I like her that way.

Yes, I like her just that way.

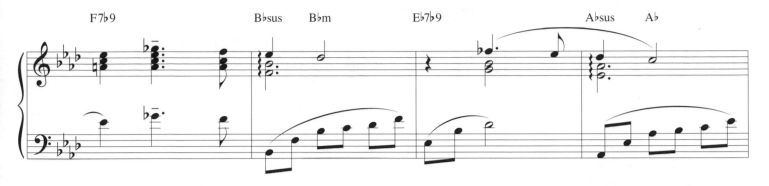

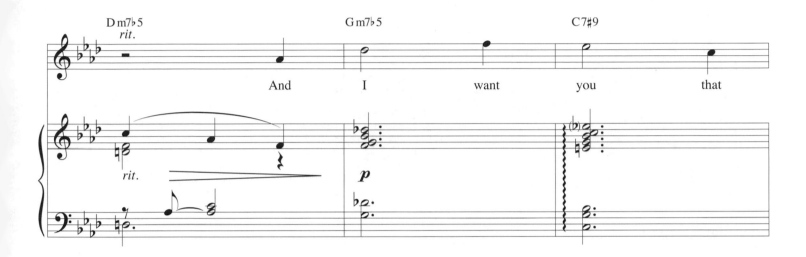

And I want you that

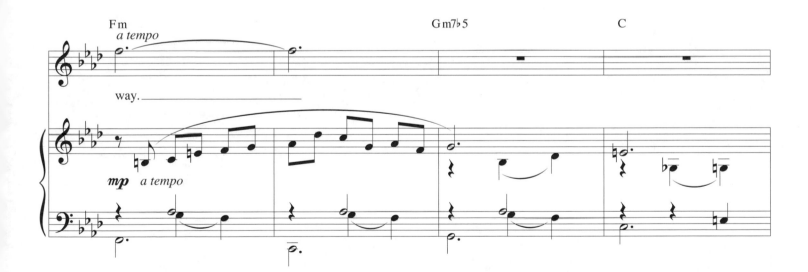

way.

SIBELLA
from *A Gentleman's Guide to Love & Murder*
audition excerpt

Music by Steven Lutvak
Lyrics by Robert L. Freedman and
Steven Lutvak

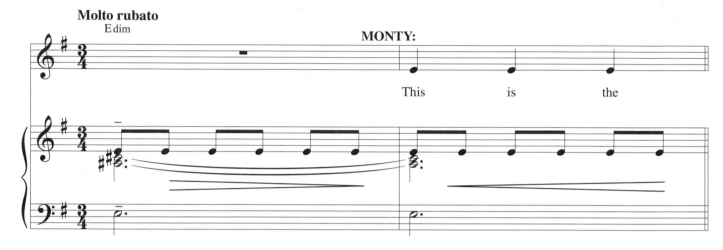

Molto rubato

MONTY:

This is the

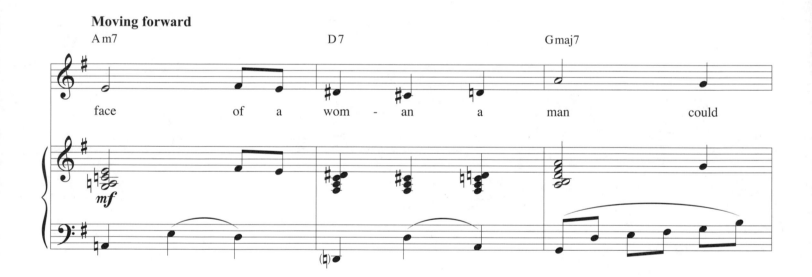

Moving forward

face   of a   wom-an   a   man   could

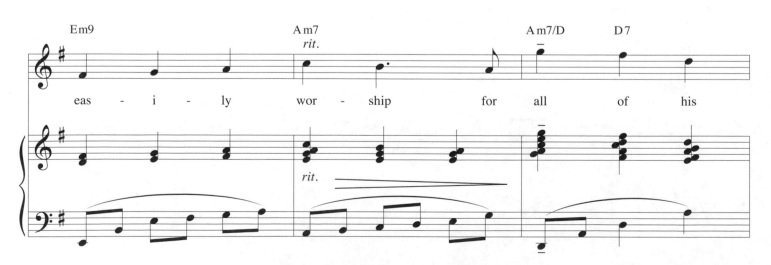

eas- i- ly   wor- ship   for   all   of   his

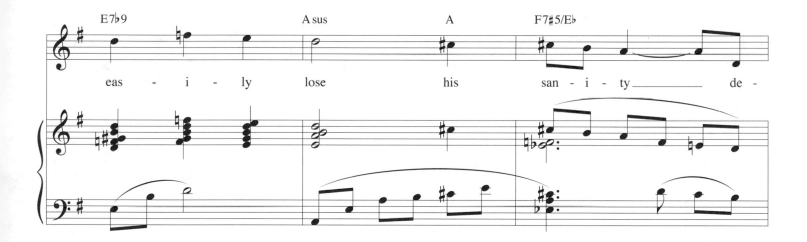

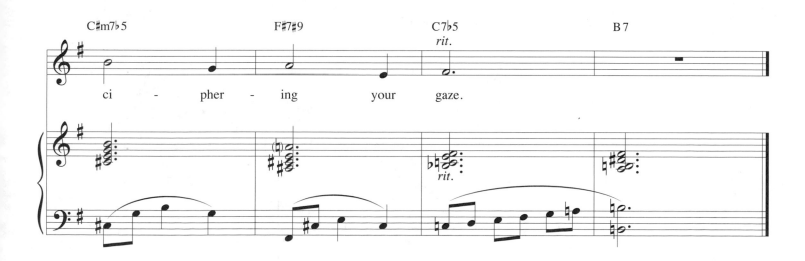

STILL
from *Anastasia*

Lyrics by Lynn Ahrens
Music by Stephen Flaherty

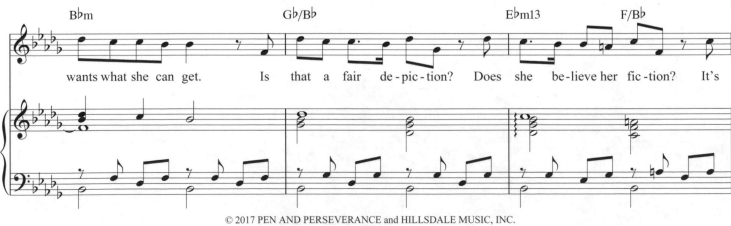

hard to know. _____ Is it in-no-cence or guile or

noth-ing but a child-ish act of will? _____ She

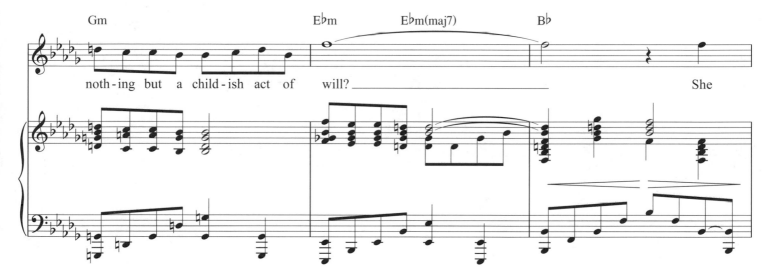

does-n't know she needs you. She will-ful-ly mis-leads you but still...

Still _____ a son be-comes a man at his

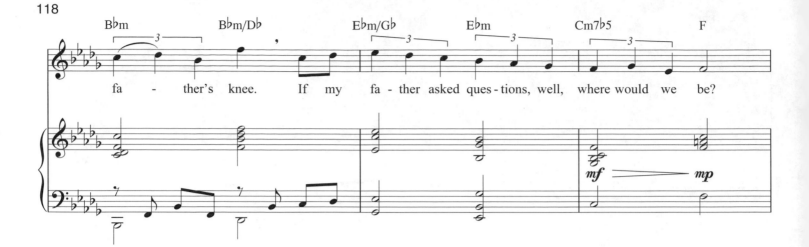

fa - ther's knee. If my fa - ther asked ques - tions, well, where would we be?

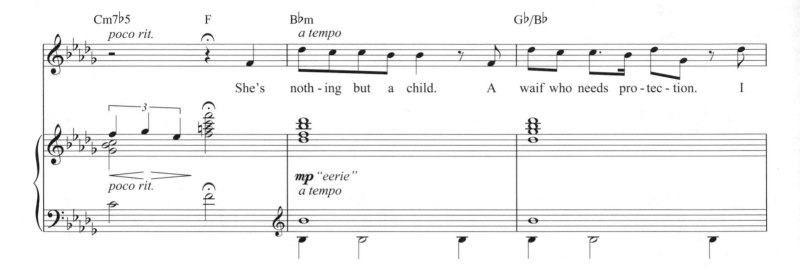

She's noth - ing but a child. A waif who needs pro - tec - tion. I

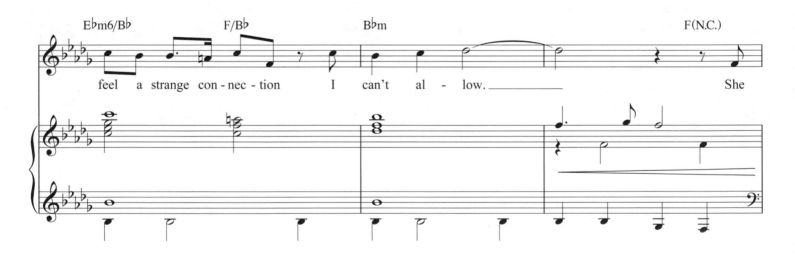

feel a strange con - nec - tion I can't al - low.____ She

says it's all a game. She trem - bles like a flow - er but in her, there's a pow - er. I

see that now._____ I am noth-ing but a man with

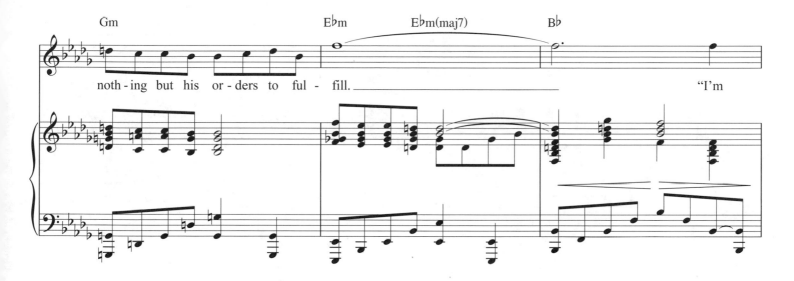

noth-ing but his or-ders to ful-fill._____ "I'm

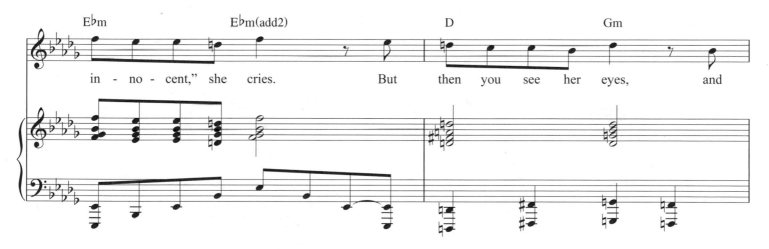

in - no - cent," she cries. But then you see her eyes, and

some-thing in them tells you that she ab - so - lute - ly lies!

Un - til your heart re - plies

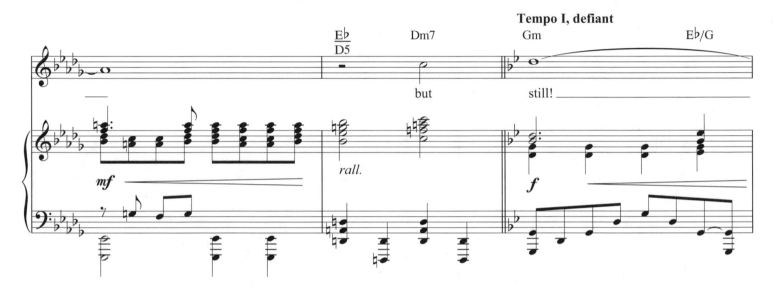

but still!

Tempo I, defiant

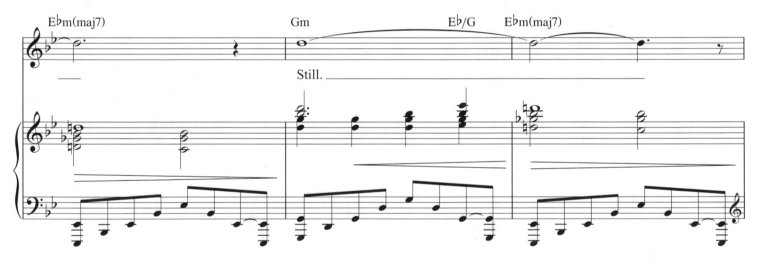

Still.

(opt.) Still.

STILL
from *Anastasia*
audition excerpt

Lyrics by Lynn Ahrens
Music by Stephen Flaherty

TAKE A CHANCE ON ME
from the Stage Musical *Little Women*

Music by Jason Howland
Lyrics by Mindi Dickstein

This is ver - y nice, such a love - ly par - ty. The mu - sic sounds so thrill - ing. ___

___ It makes a per - son feel like danc - ing. ___

(rhythmically steady)

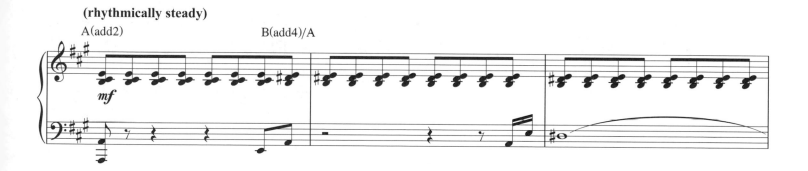

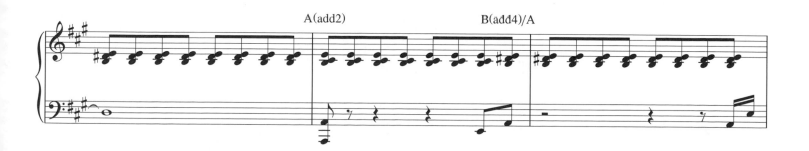

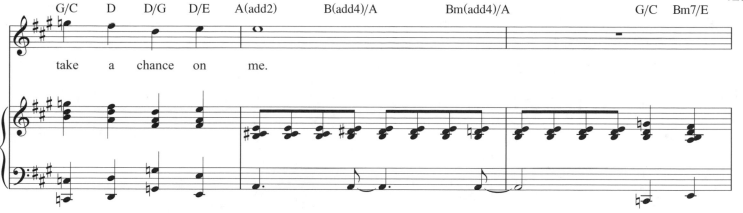

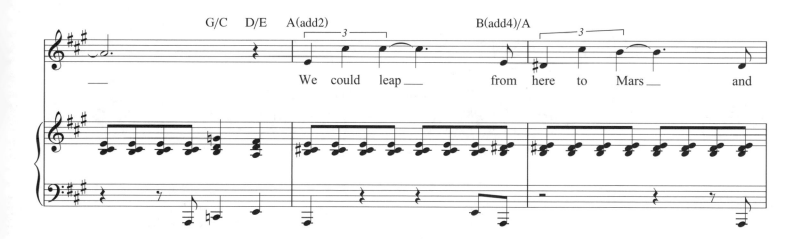

dreamed of,_____ come on, take a chance on me.

We could be such friends._____

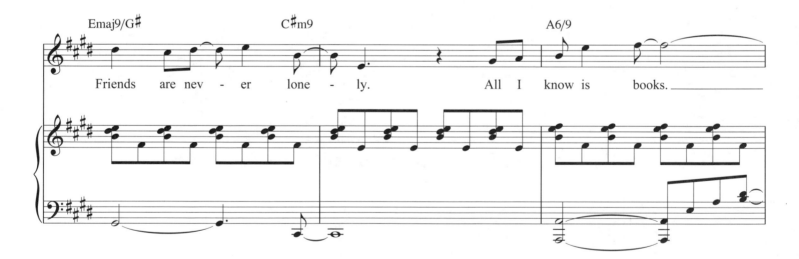

Friends are nev - er lone - ly. All I know is books._____

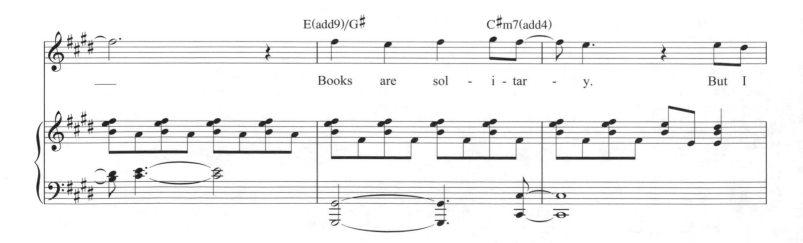

_____ Books are sol - i - tar - y. But I

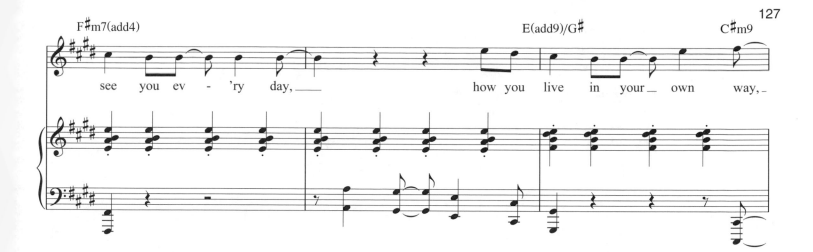

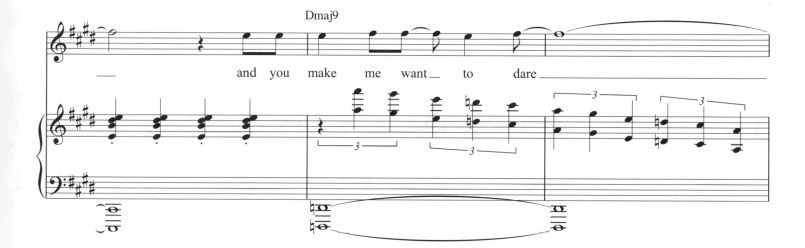

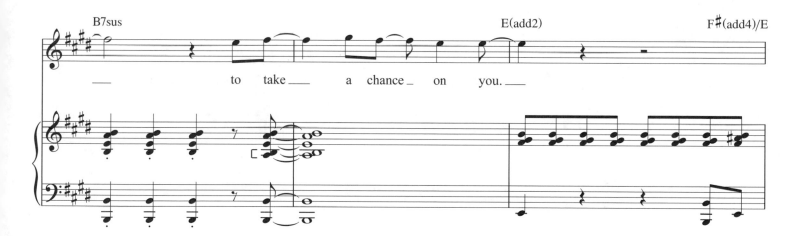

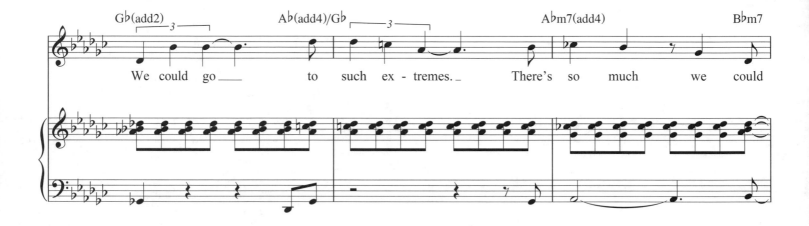

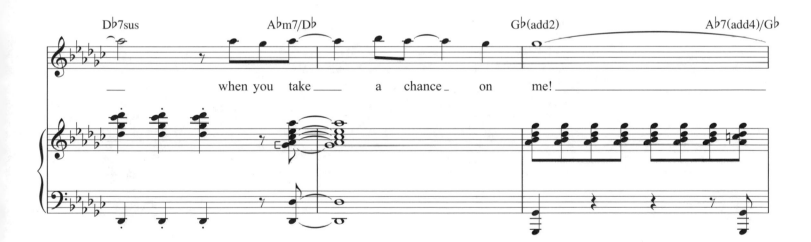

TAKE A CHANCE ON ME

from the Stage Musical *Little Women*

audition excerpt

Music by Jason Howland
Lyrics by Mindi Dickstein

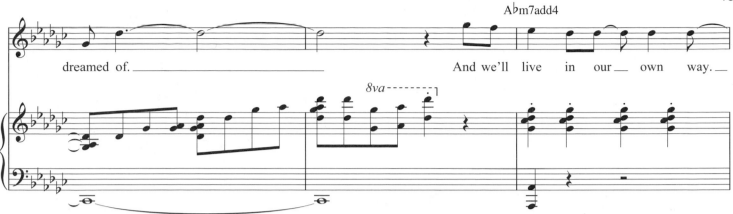

dreamed of._____ And we'll live in our___ own way.__

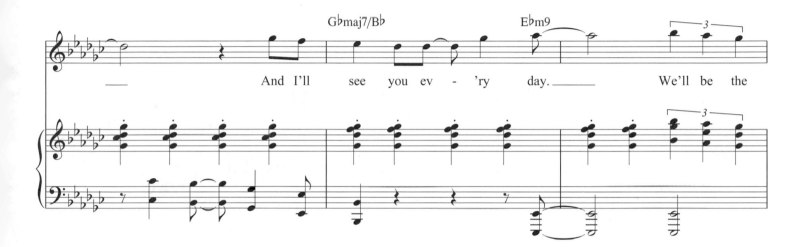

___ And I'll see you ev - 'ry day._____ We'll be the

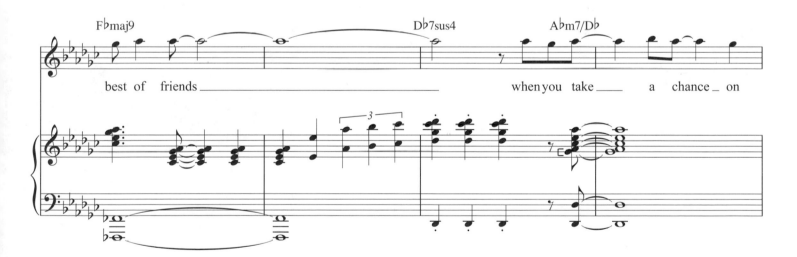

best of friends _____ when you take___ a chance_ on

me! _____

This page has been left blank to facilitate page turns.

WAVING THROUGH A WINDOW

from *Dear Evan Hansen*

Music and Lyrics by Benj Pasek
and Justin Paul

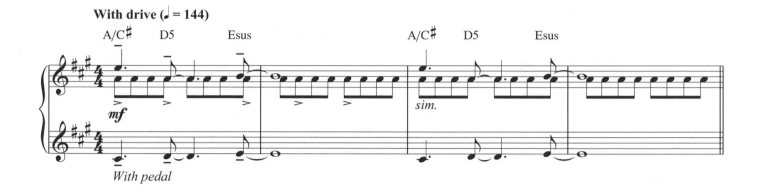

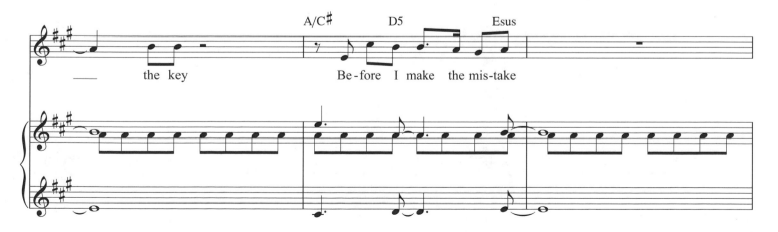

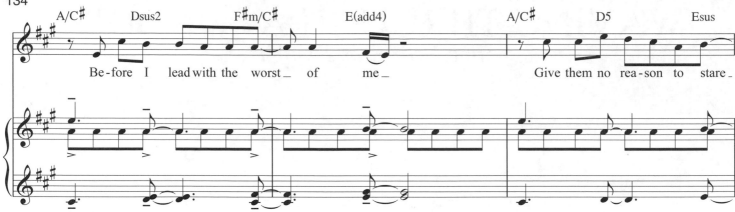

Be-fore I lead with the worst_ of me_ Give them no rea-son to stare_

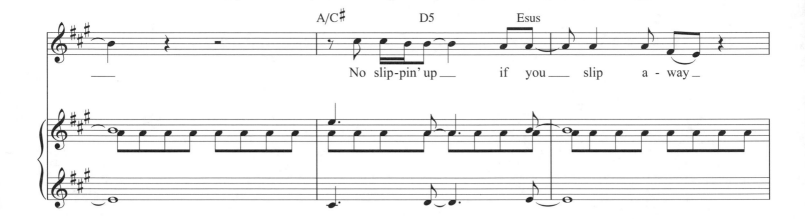

No slip-pin' up_ if you_ slip a - way_

So I got noth-in' to share No, I got noth-in' to say_

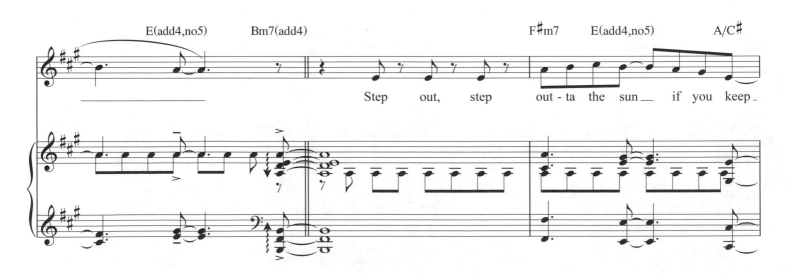

Step out, step out-ta the sun_ if you keep_

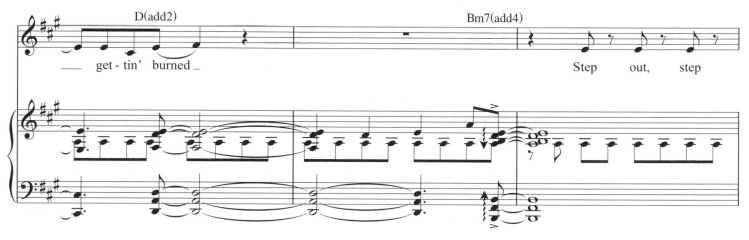

get - tin' burned __ Step out, step

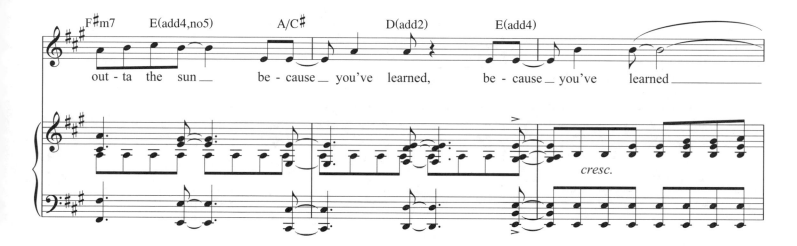

out - ta the sun __ be - cause __ you've learned, be - cause __ you've learned __

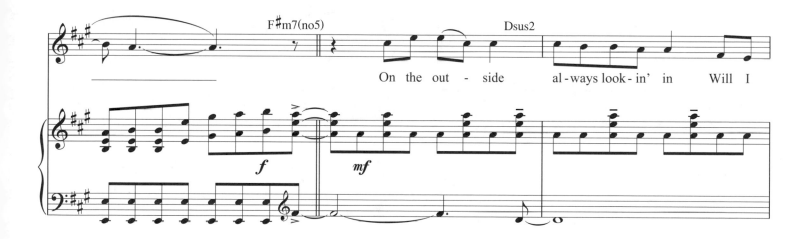

__ On the out - side al - ways look - in' in Will I

ev - er be __ more than I've al - ways been? 'Cause I'm tap - tap - tap - pin' on the

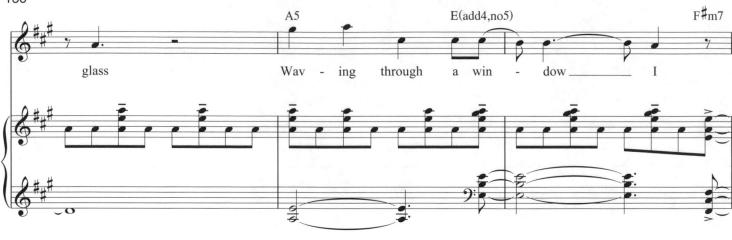

glass   Wav - ing through a win - dow ____ I

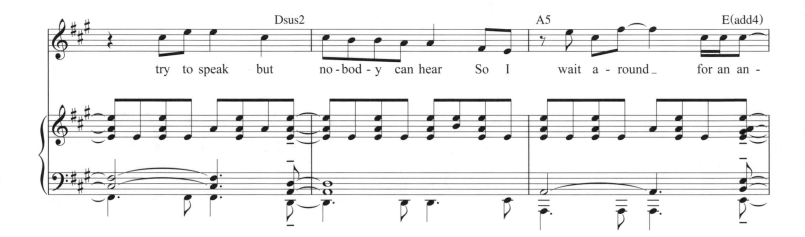

try to speak but no - bod - y can hear   So I   wait a - round_   for an an -

- swer to ap - pear   while I'm watch - watch - watch-in' peo - ple ____ pass

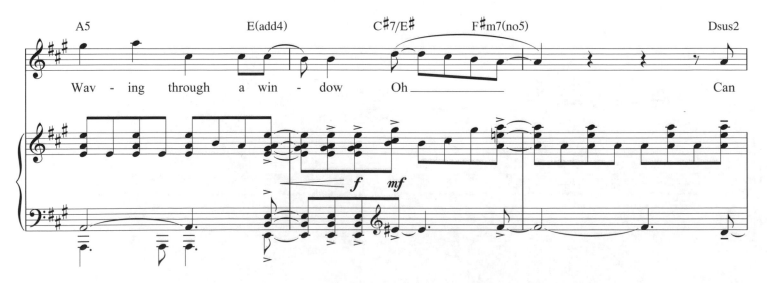

Wav - ing through a win - dow   Oh _____   Can

an-y-bod-y see?___ Is an-y-bod-y wav-ing___

back at me?___

Lift (♩ = 146)

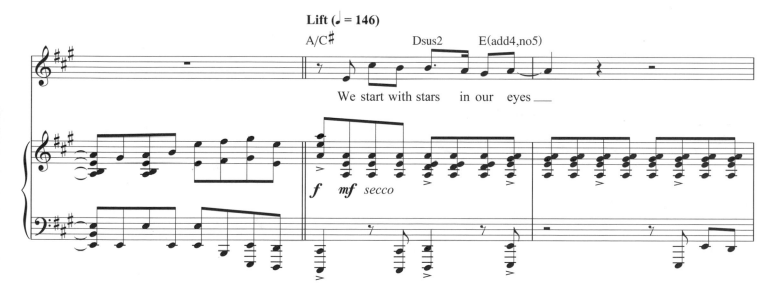

We start with stars in our eyes___

We start be-liev-in' that we___ be-long___ But ev-'ry sun___ does-n't rise___

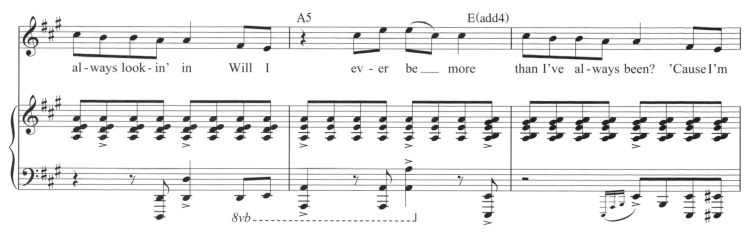

al - ways look - in' in   Will I   ev - er be __ more   than I've al - ways been? 'Cause I'm

tap - tap - tap-pin' on the __ glass _____   Wav - ing through a win-

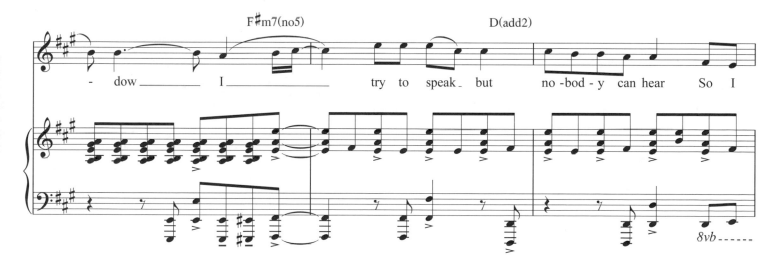

- dow _____ I _____ try to speak __ but   no-bod-y can hear   So I

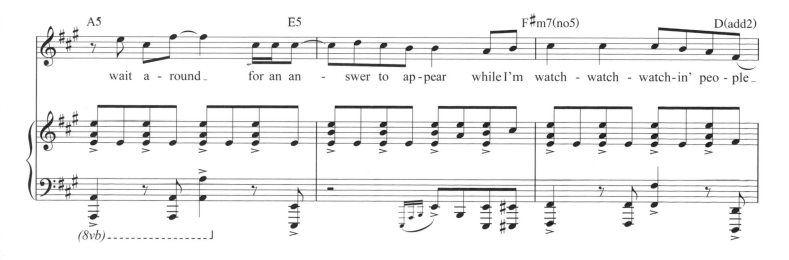

wait a - round __ for an an - swer to ap-pear   while I'm watch - watch - watch-in' peo - ple __

F#m7(no5)   A/C#   Dsus2   E(add4,no5)   F#m7(no5)

no - bod-y a - round__ do you ev - er real - ly crash or e - ven make a sound?   When you're

A/C#   Dsus2   E(add4)   F#m7   A/C#   Dsus2   E(add4)

fall - in' in a for - est   and there's no - bod-y a - round__ do you ev - er real - ly crash or e -

mf   *cresc. poco a poco*

(EVAN:)   F#m7   A/C#   Dsus2   E(add4)   F#m7

ven make a sound?__ When you're fall - in' in a for - est   and there's no - body a - round__ Do you

*COMPANY:

Ah __

Ah __

*The company may be omitted when performing this song as a solo.

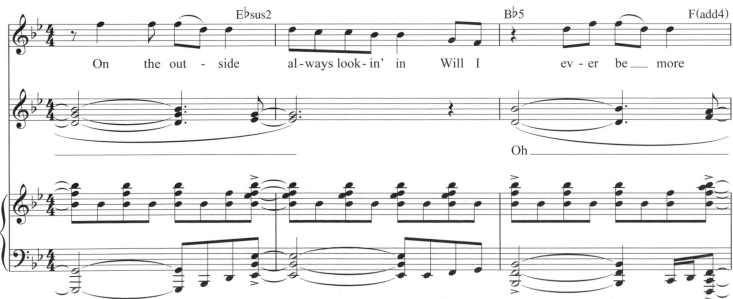

WAVING THROUGH A WINDOW

from *Dear Evan Hansen*

audition excerpt

Music and Lyrics by Benj Pasek
and Justin Paul

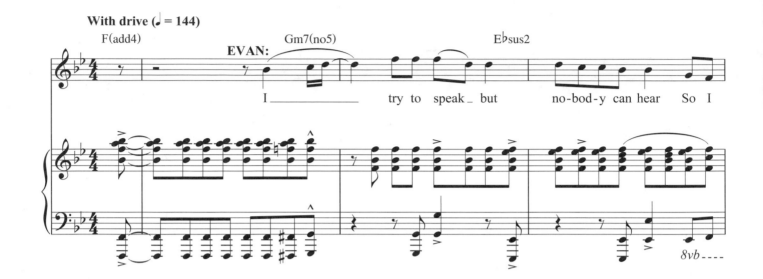

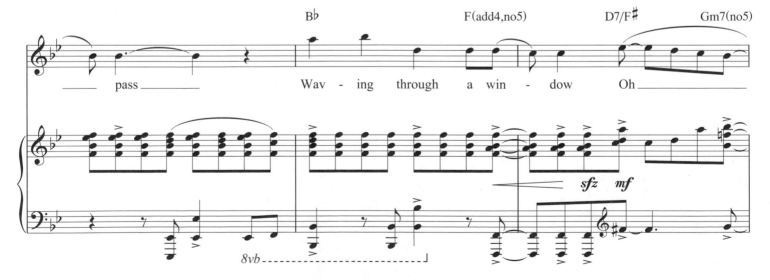

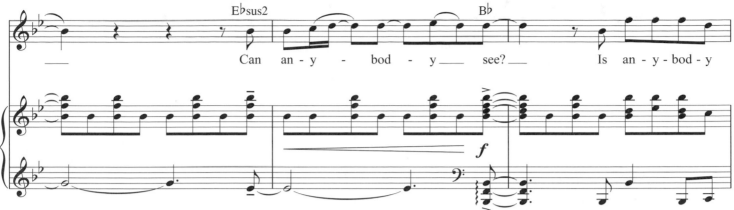

WHAT DO I NEED WITH LOVE
from *Thoroughly Modern Millie*

Music by Jeanine Tesori
Lyrics by Dick Scanlan

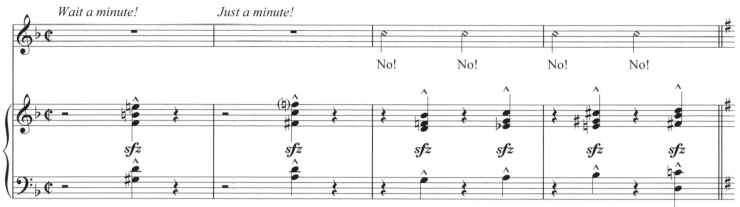

Wait a minute!   Just a minute!

No!   No!   No!   No!

A tempo - swingy, in 2

I'm a Joe with just one aim: ___ Ev-'ry night to date a dif-f'rent dame, ___

Call each one of 'em the same pet name, ___ "Hey, Ba - by."

In a row I have my ducks. ___ Loads of gals to give me loads of yucks. ___

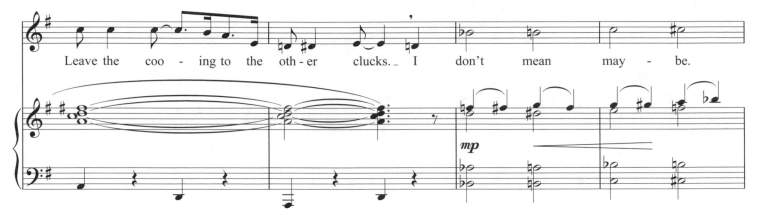

Leave the coo - ing to the oth - er clucks. __ I don't mean may - be.

Got it good. __ What do I need __ with love?

Al - ways prac - tice what I preach: __ keep temp - ta - tion out of eas - y reach. __

Stick to dolls who wash their hair in bleach, __ I'm __ hap - py.

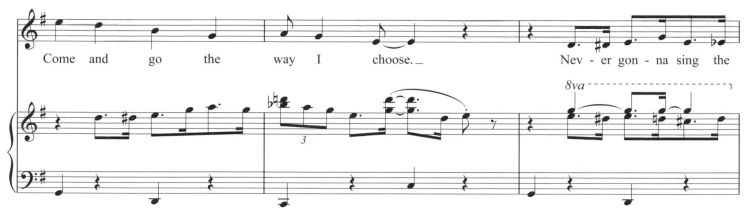

Come and go the way I choose. ___ Nev - er gon - na sing the

tied down blues. ___ Oth - er guys ___ would kill to fill my shoes. ___ No

wing - clipped sap - py! Got it good. ___ What do I need ___ with

love? ___ That was a near miss.

Talk a-bout a close shave. ___ Flirt - ed with dis - as - ter.

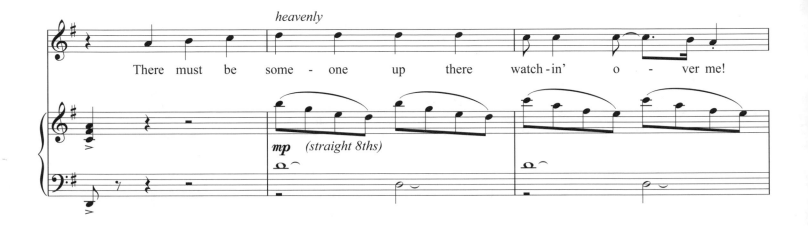

heavenly

There must be some - one up there watch-in' o - ver me!

mp *(straight 8ths)*

Talk a - bout a four-leaf - clo - ver - me. Pe - ter Rab-bit's

mf *(swing 8ths)*

miss - ing foot - sie means I roll with - out a toot - sie.

mf

Got it good.___ What do I need___ with love?_____

___ I got it good.___ What do I need___ with

Double time feel - Straight 8ths
"Jolson"

love?_____ Skip the vows and

all that rot.___ Tell the min - is - ter that "I___ do"___ not.

Bright and breez - y is the... Birds and bee - sy is the... Free and eas - y is the

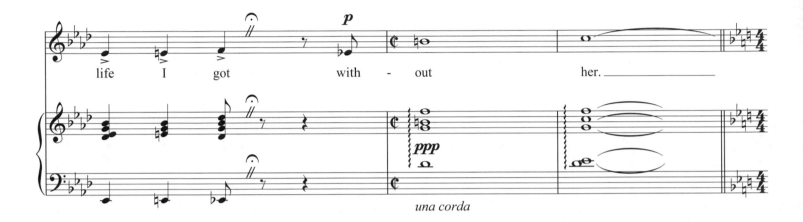

life I got with - out her.

una corda

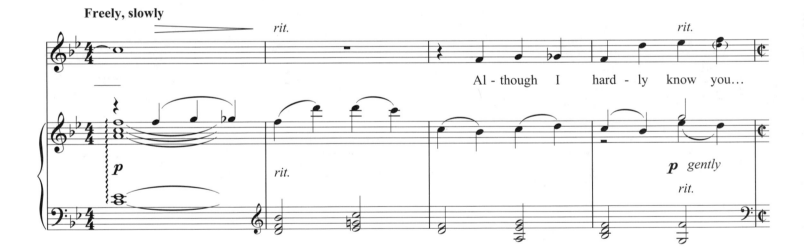

Freely, slowly

Al - though I hard - ly know you...

p gently

Swing!

What do I need with love? I

155

got it good.

Got it good. _____ I got it

bad! _____

WHAT DO I NEED WITH LOVE

from *Thoroughly Modern Millie*

audition excerpt

Music by Jeanine Tesori
Lyrics by Dick Scanlan

YOU'LL BE BACK

from *Hamilton*

Words and Music by Lin-Manuel Miranda

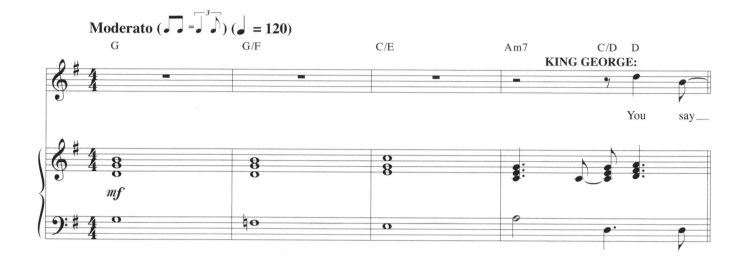

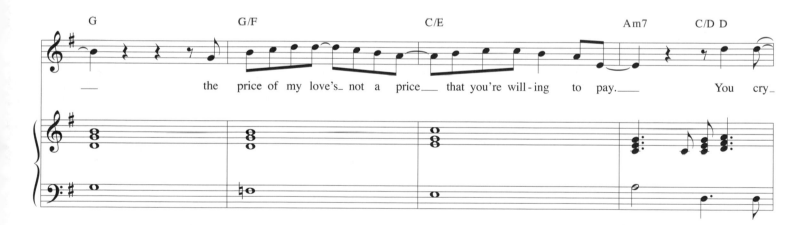

Em — G/D — Cmaj9

Re - mem - ber we made_ an ar - range - ment when you_ went a - way,

C/D — D — Em — Em/D

_ now you're mak - ing me mad._ Re - mem - ber, de - spite_ our es - trange -

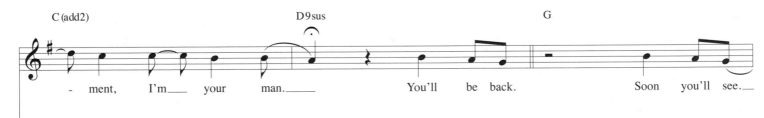

C(add2) — D9sus — G

- ment, I'm_ your man._ You'll be back. Soon you'll see._

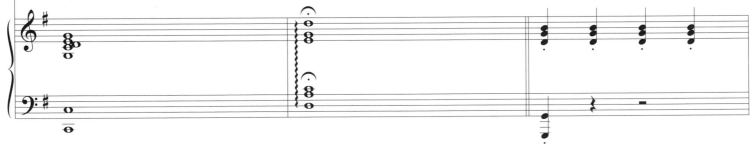

G/F — C/E — Am7 — C/D — D

_ You'll re - mem - ber you be - long to me._ You'll_ be back._

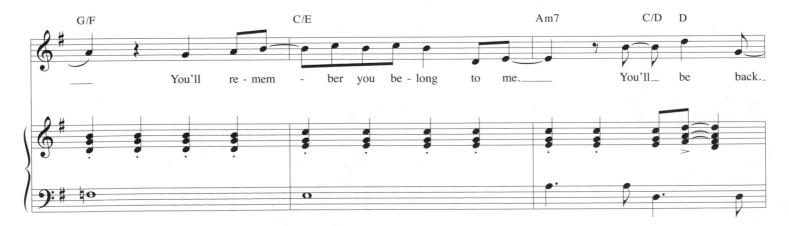

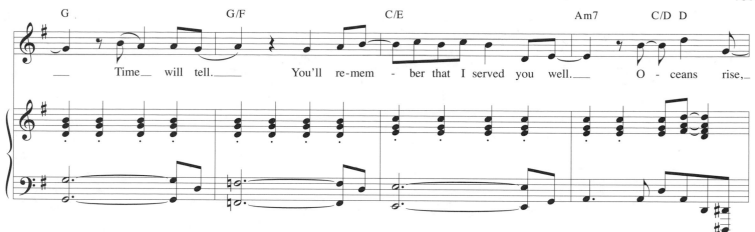

Time__ will tell.__ You'll re-mem - ber that I served you well.__ O - ceans rise,__

em - pires fall,__ we have seen__ each oth-er through it all,__ and__ when push__

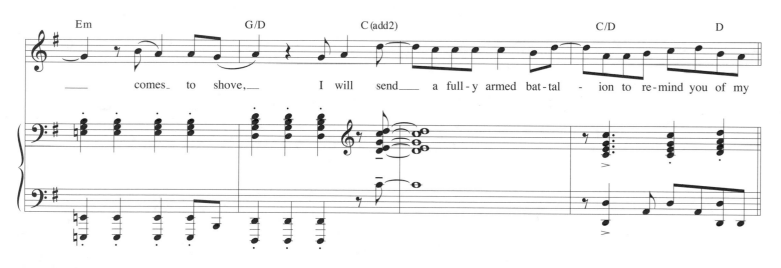

comes_ to shove,__ I will send__ a full-y armed bat-tal - ion to re-mind you of my

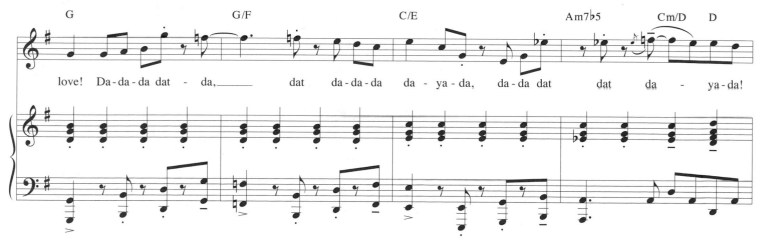

love! Da-da-da dat - da,__ dat da-da-da da-ya-da, da-da dat dat da - ya-da!

Da - da - da dat - da,_____ dat da - da - da da - ya - da, da - da dat dat da... You

say_ our love_ is drain-ing and you can't go on._____ You'll

be_ the one_ com - plain-ing when_ I am gone..._____ And

no, don't change the sub - ject 'cause you're_ my fav-'rite sub - ject. My

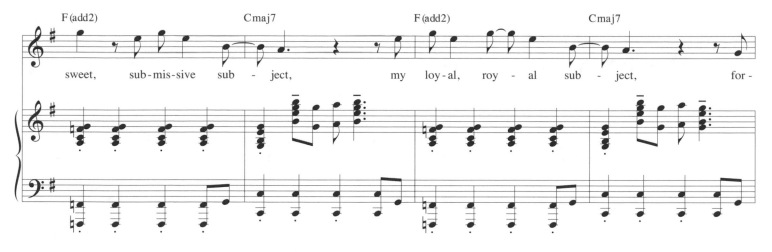

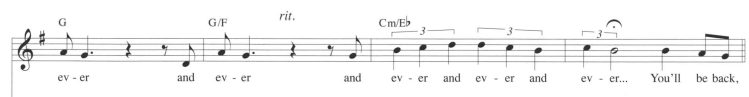

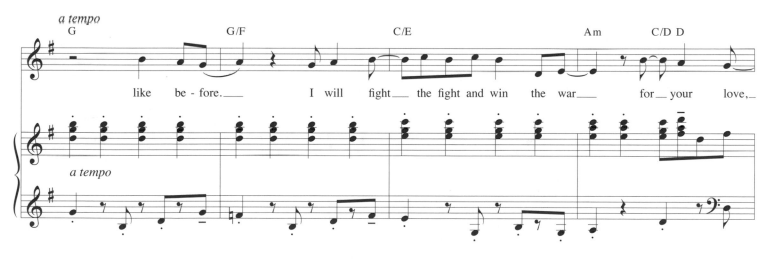

I'll go mad, so don't throw a-way this thing we had. 'Cause when push

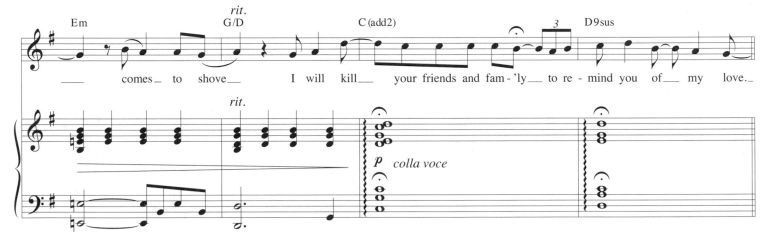

comes to shove I will kill your friends and fam-'ly to re-mind you of my love.

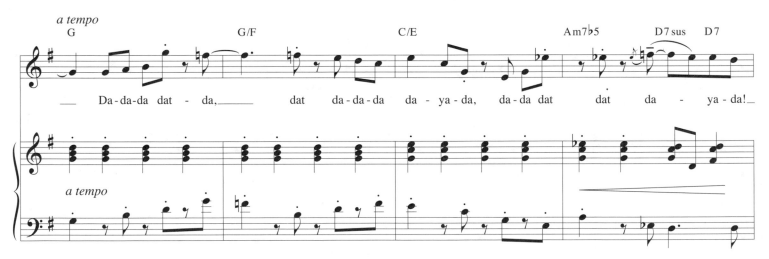

Da-da-da dat-da, dat da-da-da da-ya-da, da-da dat dat da-ya-da!

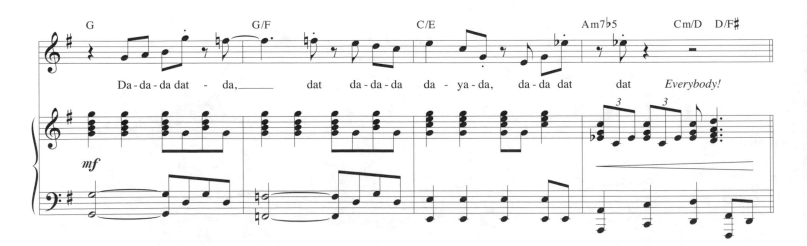

Da-da-da dat-da, dat da-da-da da-ya-da, da-da dat dat *Everybody!*

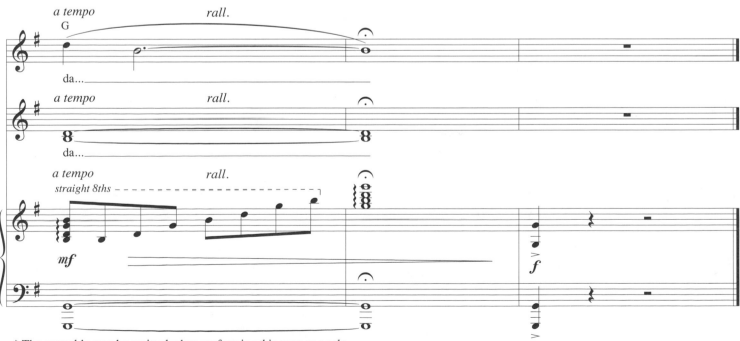

* The ensemble may be omitted when performing this song as a solo.

YOU'LL BE BACK

from *Hamilton*

audition exceprt

Words and Music by Lin-Manuel Miranda

Moderato ♩ = 120

KING GEORGE:

You say___ our love___ is

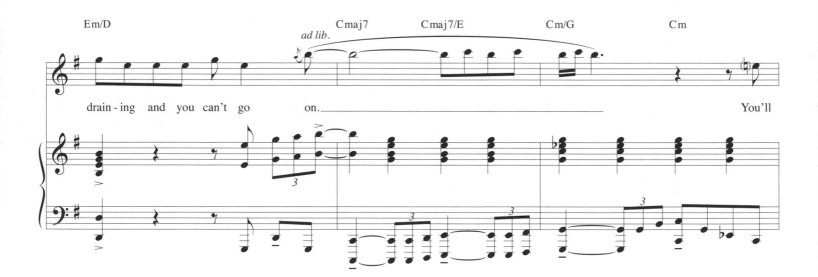

drain-ing and you can't go on.___ You'll

be___ the one___ com-plain-ing when___ I am gone...

HOW TO USE HAL LEONARD ONLINE AUDIO

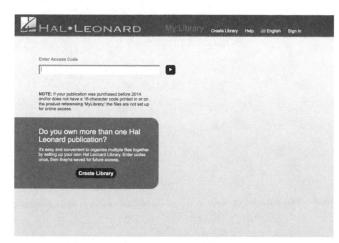

Because of the changing use of media, and the fact that fewer people are using CDs, we have made a shift to companion audio accessible online. In many cases, rather than a book with CD, we now have a book with an access code for online audio, including performances, accompaniments or diction lessons. Each copy of each book has a unique access code. We call this Hal Leonard created system "My Library." It's simple to use.

Go to www.halleonard.com/mylibrary and enter the unique access code found on page one of a relevant book/audio package.

The audio tracks can be streamed or downloaded. If you download the tracks on your computer, you can add the files to a CD or to your digital music library, and use them anywhere without being online. See below for comments about Apple and Android mobile devices.

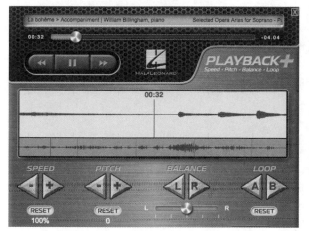

There are some great benefits to the My Library system. *Playback+* is exclusive to Hal Leonard, and when connected to the Internet with this multi-functional audio player you can:

• Change tempo without changing pitch
• Transpose to any key

Optionally, you can create a My Library account, and store all the companion audio you have purchased there. Access your account online at any time, from any device, by logging into your account at www.halleonard.com/mylibrary. Technical help may be found at www.halleonard.com/mylibrary/help/

Apple/iOS

Question: On my iPad and iPhone, the Download links just open another browser tab and play the track. How come this doesn't really download?

Answer: The Safari iOS browser will not allow you to download audio files directly in iTunes or other apps. There are several ways to work around this:

• You can download normally on your desktop computer, saving the files to iTunes. Then, you can sync your iOS device directly to your computer, or sync your iTunes content using an iCloud account.

• There are many third-party apps which allow you to download files from websites into the app's own file manager for easy retrieval and playback.

Android

Files are always downloaded to the same location, which is a folder usually called "Downloads" (this may vary slightly depending on what browser is used (Chrome, Firefox, etc)). Chrome uses a system app called "Downloads" where files can be accessed at any time. Firefox and some other browsers store downloaded files within a "Downloads" folder in the browser itself.

Recently-downloaded files can be accessed from the Notification bar; swiping down will show the downloaded files as a new "card", which you tap on to open. Opening a file depends on what apps are installed on the Android device. Audio files are opened in the device's default audio app. If a file type does not have a default app assigned to it, the Android system alerts the user.